A
College
for
This Community

A
College
for
This Community

A History of the Local Colleges Antecedent
to Volunteer State Community College
Gallatin, Tennessee

By Walter T. Durham

Library of Congress Catalogue Card Number: 74-81814

MANUFACTURED BY THE PARTHENON PRESS AT
NASHVILLE, TENNESSEE, UNITED STATES OF AMERICA

To all who care about learning.

CONTENTS

LIST OF ILLUSTRATIONS

Photographs No. 3, 6, 7, 9, 11, 12 and 13 by Tippy Crutcher.

PREFACE

One of my earliest boyhood memories is of spending hot summer afternoons in a pasture near our Gallatin home and playing in the shade of the two large remnants of the Pythian College cornerstone. Why and how the original limestone block, some six feet high and four feet square at the base, had been transported forty years earlier to the center of that farm lot were questions that did not seem to bother me. I remember, however, that I was disturbed by the fact that it had been broken and the contents of its tiny box vault removed by persons unknown. Time and again I unsuccessfully examined the stone fragments hoping to find the secret to the cornerstone's violation.

When construction of the first buildings at Volunteer State Community College was completed in 1972, several local people expressed interest in establishing on the campus some tangible evidence of Gallatin's long struggle to secure and sustain a successful institute of higher learning. When I suggested using the Pythian College cornerstone for this purpose, it was promptly visited and purchased by representatives of the Gallatin Lions Club. The smaller half of the huge cut limestone block, on which is embossed the date of its dedication and the emblem of the Knights of Pythias, was removed to the Vol State campus. The larger portion and some small fragments were left in place near the rear line fence of a residence on Ross Avenue in a Gallatin subdivision created from the pasture lot of my childhood.

The gift of the stone to the college by the Lions Club immediately prompted a barrage of questions. What is it? Where did it come from? What was the Pythian College? What happened to it? Were there any other colleges worthy of the name in Gallatin? What about local colleges in the old days?

This book is in answer to these questions. It is the story of the predecessors and the would-be predecessors of Volunteer State Community College.

Frequently a writer of history finds that he has received assistance from so many sources that a faithful acknowledgment to all

ix

would be as lengthy as the book itself. This is one of those times. I must, however, recognize that without the approval of my wife Anna and my business associate John Phillips this work would never have been attempted. And without the assistance of my secretary Glenda Vanatta it would never have been completed. Personnel at the Tennessee State Library and Archives, Nashville, have been patient and helpful. Mrs. Nell House McDonald, Head Librarian of the Edward Ward Carmack Sumner County Library, Gallatin, Attorney Nathan Harsh, and Judge Ernest Pellegrin have been especially helpful as we have moved the book from typescript to market.

WALTER T. DURHAM

September 1, 1974

INTRODUCTION

The creation of Volunteer State Community College at Gallatin has fulfilled the heretofore frustrated dreams of local partisans of education—dreams that can be dated back to the early nineteenth century when attempts were first made to develop an institution of higher learning for the area. In the years between 1838 and 1969, when the Tennessee Higher Education Commission voted to locate its latest in a series of junior colleges in Sumner County, people of the community had witnessed the rise and fall of four colleges, had seen the two most ambitious educational undertakings of the period die in the agony of birth, and had watched with shocked disbelief as the voters of the county vetoed a referendum that would have made possible the location of the Middle Tennessee State Normal College near Gallatin.

The decision to locate Volunteer State Community College at Gallatin, reached after extensive research and careful evaluation of the area, was based in part on the community's expressed interest in becoming the site of a state-operated junior college. The county of Sumner had early announced its intent to comply with the terms of the enabling act by furnishing the 100-acre campus site and by supplying the sum of $250,000 to aid in construction of the initial buildings. The city of Gallatin had pledged its support by agreeing to extend all utilities and requisite municipal services to the school and later had extended its corporation limits to include the campus area. And, all the while, a special committee of the Gallatin Chamber of Commerce had been producing research data to demonstrate the size and quality of the pool of young people and adults from whom the college's students would be drawn.

Any doubt that Volunteer State Community College had been created at the right place at the right time was dispelled when the first enrollment period ended with a beginning student body of 600. At the beginning of its second year the number of students stood at 1,408. It is projected that the student body will continue to grow until it reaches a total of approximately 2,000, a size at which it is expected to become relatively stable.

1

With the campus not yet ready for occupancy in September 1971, the beginning student body of 600 attended classes wherever space was available in Gallatin. The college administrative headquarters were temporarily located in the old Cordell Hull Hotel Building. Space for classrooms was made available at the First Baptist Church, the First United Methodist Church, the First Presbyterian Church, the East Main Church of Christ, the National Guard Armory, and the Gallatin Junior High School.

When construction of campus buildings was completed about December 31, 1971, the college moved to its present location. Classes were conducted on this the permanent campus beginning with the winter quarter, January, 1972.

Dr. Hal Ramer, Assistant Commissioner for Higher Education in the Tennessee State Department of Education from 1963 to 1970 and, earlier, Assistant to the President of Ohio State University, became the first President of Volunteer State in July, 1970. Under his leadership the college directs its services primarily to citizens in the counties of Cheatham, Davidson, Macon, Wilson, Robertson, Smith, Trousdale, and Sumner.

The busy college and the presence of its students and faculty members in the community are curiously reminiscent of earlier times when local folk first sought to establish schools of higher learning to educate their young at home in preference to sending them to schools located in such distant places as Baltimore or Philadelphia. Wirt College, its name later changed to Enon College; Howard Female College; Neophogen Male and Female College; and Tullatuskee Normal College were institutions in the area authorized to confer degrees and which, for the most part, offered course work the equivalent of today's community colleges, and including, in one case, courses leading to a degree in law.

The Isaac Franklin Institute and the Pythian University were the two local schools representing the most ambitious educational undertakings of the nineteenth century. The stories of the failure of both are told against the background of each institution's unique birth experience. The local voters' irrevocable decision to stand aside from any opportunity to bring Middle Tennessee State Normal to Sumner County, although incredible in retrospect, was

2

largely the result of anxiety about the state of public finances, locally crippled by the recent failure of a railroad construction project that had been funded by Sumner County bonds.

Before the advent of public schools in grades one through twelve, much of the energy and money available from local citizens was, of necessity, directed into the operation of private and community schools and academies. There is no doubt that institutions of higher learning suffered from the competition for both moral and financial support.

While this study deals only with institutions that offered courses and degrees beyond high school levels, it is important to understand that the number of private and community schools was legion. Many existed for a few months or a few years and passed into oblivion only to be replaced by others. Their names were frequently as colorful as their futures were uncertain. An incomplete list of schools that existed in Sumner County before the present era of public schools includes the following: Bethpage School, Bledsoe Academy, Gallatin School, Gallatin Female Academy, Gallatin Male Seminary, Hartsville Academy, Hartsville Female Institute, Independence School, Liberty High School, Littleton Academy, Lodabar Academy, Madison Academy, McElwrath School, McKendree Academy, Mt. Zion Academy, New Hope Baptist School, Pleasant Grove School, Rural Academy, Shallow Ford Academy, Sumner County High School, Sumner-Robertson Normal, Sumner Training School, Transmontania Academy, Troutt's Academy, Van Buren School, Station Camp Academy, Masonic Male High School of Gallatin, Pine Ford Academy, Tennessee High School, Union High School of Gallatin, Sylvan Academy, Cairo Academy, Central Academy, New Salem School House, Mrs. Garrett's Female Seminary, Wallace's School House, Western Military Institute, The Shackle Island School, Sumner Academy, Portland Seminary, Pericles Academy, Sunnyside School, Boyers School, Edmondson Seminary, and Simpson Seminary.

CHAPTER I

WIRT COLLEGE

THE ORIGINS OF the first school in Sumner County to be chartered by the State of Tennessee as an institution of higher learning with the power to confer the Bachelors and Masters degrees are found in the opening of Wirt Seminary in 1838. Located eleven miles east of Gallatin and five miles west of Hartsville near the present intersection of U.S. Highway 231 and State Highway 25, Wirt Seminary opened its doors under the proprietorship of the teaching partners Thomas M. Patterson and Thomas M. Fite.

For whom was the seminary named? No trace of an answer to this question has been discovered in the advertisements and announcements published by the school during its lifetime nor in the charter that it received from the legislature in 1843. It is speculated that the institution was named to memorialize the life of William Wirt, a man of letters and Attorney General of the United States during the administration of President James Monroe. A Virginian, Wirt became a Whig and was among those who opposed Jackson's candidacy for President in 1828. In 1832 he accepted the nomination of the Anti-Mason party as its candidate for President with the expectation that the Whigs would join in a united front against Old Hickory. The effort to unite the opposition to Jackson failed to materialize, however, and Wirt was left an unwilling candidate for the highest office in the land. In 1834 while living in Washington, D.C., he died at the age of 62.

A newspaper announcement appearing in the Gallatin *Union* June 22, 1838, stated that examinations for Wirt Seminary's first session, which had apparently started in January or February, would be held July 19 with the second session of school set to commence on the Monday following. Readers were advised that Wirt was a boys school and that boarding accommodations for students could be arranged in private homes near the seminary. A board of visitors had been created by the proprietors and its members drawn from the prominent citizens of the surrounding countryside. The members of the board in 1838 were J. Anthony, John Wilks, Joel Algood, Peter Wynne, Lewis Haynie, Charles M. White, W. W. Young, J. W. H. Townsend, John Wiseman, Robert White, and S. W. Malone.

At least two Wirt students had joined in the political rally at Hartsville honoring James K. Polk in the late autumn of his 1838 campaign for governor. While the identity of both young men was withheld from readers of the Gallatin *Union* of November 16, 1838, the report of the festivities included their proposed toasts along with those of the political leaders of the day. One of the students, identified, like his companion, only as "a student of Wirt Seminary," made bold use of sarcasm in his toast: "Henry Clay. The most excellent fence rider of Kentucky, may he, after the year 1840, fall on one side or the other, and there lie dormant!" The other Wirt student offered a genial toast to candidate Polk that was concluded with a pun at the expense of Polk's adversary, Newton Cannon. He said, "James K. Polk, a true and genuine patriot of Tennessee; may he be enabled to destroy all powder that may chance to fall into the dark cavity of the horrid Cannon."

Mail service to Wirt Seminary was provided by Lewis Haynie, U.S. Postmaster at nearby Green Garden, from 1838 to 1840. On February 13, 1840, the post office at Green Garden was discontinued and a U.S. Post Office was set up at Wirt Seminary. Lewis Haynie became postmaster at Wirt Seminary and served until he was replaced by Thomas M. Patterson, one of the proprietors of the school, on November 13, 1841.[1]

The school's operations seem to have been continued on a regular basis. An announcement that the ninth session would begin in January, 1842, strongly indicates that two sessions had been held each year since the opening in early 1838. The ninth session call was signed by Thomas M. Patterson and C. B. Patterson.[2]

By 1843, the proprietors of Wirt Seminary determined to have

---

[1] *United States Postal Records,* National Archives and Records Service.

[2] Nashville *Union,* December 17, 1841. Thomas M. Fite, co-founder with T. M. Patterson, had left Wirt by this time and C. B. Patterson had become his brother's partner.

the institution incorporated and chartered under the name of Wirt College with authority to confer the Bachelor of Arts and Master of Arts degrees. The state legislature, meeting at Nashville, promptly granted their request and passed "An Act to incorporate Wirt College in the county of Sumner."

Reciting pertinent facts dealing with the school's background, the Act declared:

> Whereas, a literary institution located in Sumner County, Tennessee, called Wirt Seminary, has been in successful operation for the past six years, the founders and proprietors of which have erected extensive, commodius and costly buildings, and have supplied the institution with apparatus and other requisites for the advancement of literature and science, its continued prosperity and present flourishing condition being attributable alone to individual enterprise, unaided by Legislative authority, and for the encouragement of such enterprise and the further promotion of the cause of education.
>
> Section 1. Be it enacted by the General Assembly of the State of Tennessee, that Wirt Seminary in Sumner county shall hereafter be known and called by the name of Wirt College, and shall enjoy all the rights, privileges, liberties, exemptions, dignities and immunities enjoyed by any literary institution in this State.
>
> Section 2. Be it enacted, that T. M. Patterson, C. B. Patterson, and W. K. Patterson, the preceptors and proprietors, shall compose the faculty of said College, with the power of appointing other professors when necessary; and they and their successors are hereby constituted, and shall forever hereafter be, a body corporate and politic to be known in law by the name of the Faculty of Wirt College, and shall have succession for a period of five hundred years, and a common seal.

The college's corporate structure was outlined in Section 3 of the Act. In Section 4, the President and Faculty were empowered to confer "the degrees of Bachelor of Arts and Master of Arts on any student, or any other person, who may possess the requisite moral and intellectual attainments, and any other degrees known and conferred by any college or University in the United States." [3]

---

[3] *Acts passed at the First Session of the Twenty-Fifth General Assembly of the State of Tennessee, 1843-44* (Nashville: L. Gifford and E. G. Eastman, Printers, 1844), Chapter XXXIX, p. 44 et seq.

With the seminary now advanced to college status, the membership of the board of visitors was impressively enlarged. The board included, in 1843, "H. B. Hill, J. Anthony, E. S. Payne, J. H. Patterson, William Read, J. B. Dickerson, J. L. Swaney, William Hall, M. Duffy, A. R. Wynne, G. C. Crenshaw, W. L. Malone, J. Saunders, S. Rickman, R. Jackson, William Goodall, H. Bate, T. Mosely, P. W. Stone, C. Hart, G. Brown, J. D. Bond, S. Debow, J. M. Jetton, J. W. Locke, N. Crenshaw and J. Algood." [4]

The board later had officers, but no records of the board, its officers and activities are known to have been preserved. The names of S. B. F. C. Barr, president, and J. M. Burney, secretary, appeared in a brief announcement in the Nashville *Union,* April 18, 1847.

The Post Office Department took due note of the changes at Wirt and changed the official post office designation to Wirt College February 26, 1844, and on the same date reappointed Thomas M. Patterson to serve as postmaster. [5]

In August, 1849, during the cholera epidemic in Middle Tennessee, the administrators of Wirt College posted notice that their institution was soon to begin its twelfth year. Referring obliquely to the epidemic, the announcement cited the school's record of 12 years of uninterrupted good health for its students and boasted that its location was "far removed from scenes of dissipation or places of public resort except churches." College courses of ten months duration were offered by professors William K. Patterson and H. R. Ring. A student paid board and tuition charges of $100 for the period. [6]

Sometime in the mid 1840's the college had entered into a contract with one Benjamin Pierce to provide board and lodging for its boarding students. In 1849, however, Wirt College re-entered the boarding and lodging business by purchasing from Pierce "for the use and benefit of the boarding and lodging department of Wirt College, thirty beds and furniture, six head of horses, twelve milch cows and calves, two yokes of oxen, two hundred head of

---

[4] *Ibid.*
[5] *United States Postal Records.*
[6] Nashville *Daily Union,* August 17, 1849.

hogs, all (his) household and kitchen furniture together with the stock of Provisions now on hand." [7]

In 1850, students were sought to enroll in five-month courses for which tuition, board and lodging charges were $50. A newspaper notice made a strong claim for Wirt College: "It is predominantly the Peoples' College, without endowments it has educated more destitute young men than the best endowed institutions in the state, within the same period of time." The government and morality of the school were designated for special comment: "Government—Justice and Benevolence kiss each other. Morality—Let each student come prepared with a Bible. It will be studied." [8]

Within the next year financial adversity was to overtake Wirt College. While the details of Wirt's last months have not been preserved, it must be assumed that the college, like most other schools of its day, could not generate sufficient funds to continue its operation. In 1851[9] the Enon Association of United Baptists purchased the college and its "property at a very reduced price and commenced a very flourishing school" which was called Enon College.[10] The Enon Association, composed of member churches located principally in Sumner, Macon, and Smith Counties, was joined in the sponsorship of Enon College in 1852 by the Salem Association of United Baptists from the Counties of Wilson, Warren, and Rutherford.[11] The Salem Association elected eleven trustees to serve the college: J. R. Aseworth, Jr., H. T. Rucks, P. Anderson, Thos. Fisher, John Chambers, W. T. Cartwright, Rev. J. Powell, Rev. J. W. Bowen, V. Campton, Rev. E. W. Haile, and William Swet.[12]

With Enon Association records missing for the years prior to 1866, and Enon College records seemingly nonexistent, the story

---

[7] *Sumner County Records* (cited hereafter as SCR), *Deed Book #21*, p. 356.

[8] Nashville *Daily Centre-State American*, July 23, 1850.

[9] J. H. Grimes, *History of Middle Tennessee Baptists* (Nashville: Baptist and Reflector, 1902), p. 299.

[10] *Minutes of the Twenty-Ninth Annual Session of the Salem Association of United Baptists, September 19-21, 1852* (McMinnville, Tennessee: The Enterprise Office, 1852), p. 3.

[11] *Ibid.*

[12] *Ibid.*, p. 4.

of the school would be lost except for the carefully preserved minutes of the annual meetings of the Salem Association. When the Salem Association met in September, 1853, the committee on Enon College reported that "the institution is in flourishing condition . . . its prospects are flattering." They further reported: "In the estimation of the Board of Trustees, an endowment of $10,000 is necessary to the permanent establishment, and certain property of the college. As this Association has an equal interest with Enon in the prosperity of the institution, they ask us to sanction the endowment means." [13]

Both Salem and Enon Associations agreed to try to raise the desired endowment, but their efforts were not productive. The Salem Association committee on Enon College reported to the annual meeting in September, 1854:

> We regret to inform you that this Institution is in a languishing condition. From a communication . . . by the resident Trustees . . . we learn that the efforts sanctioned by Enon and Salem Associations to raise an endowment fund has resulted in a failure.

Money problems were piling up. The report continued:

> . . . the institution has been a sinking business from the beginning, and . . . there is now an unliquidated debt of $2,500.00 hanging over it, and no means to pay. . . .

The committee recommended that the Association face the unpleasant facts. Its report continued:

> The question . . . at this point is what shall be done? Not doubting but that there have been errors committed in the past, which have led to these disastrous results. Your committee are impressed with the uselessness of indulging in attempted criminations of the past. This debt must be paid and honourably discharged. Plighted faith, moral obligation . . . require it. The honor of two Associations is at stake, and every highminded, honorable man prefers death to dishonor.
> This debt must be paid, but how paid? By raising the money at once and securing the property, or by selling the property for what

---

[13] *Minutes of the Thirteenth Annual Session of the Salem Association of United Baptists, September 17-20, 1853* (McMinnville, Tennessee: The Enterprise Office, 1853), p. 6.

it will bring, and then raise the balance? Your committee recommend that an effort be made to raise the money and pay the debt....[14]

A year later, the future of Enon College appeared dark indeed. The Salem Association gathered at Lebanon, Tennessee, in 1855 and heard the report of its Enon College committee:

Enon College . . . has gone down in disaster. Referring to the report of last year, we adopt its sentiments in full, so far as the moral obligation resting upon us to discharge the debt is concerned. While we condemn the course of O. J. Fisk in bringing suit against our Trustees, and disavow, on our part the existence of any legal obligation, we recommend the following resolution:

Resolved, that this Association appoint a committee to meet a committee on the part of Enon Association, to devise some plan to raise a fund to liquidate the existing debt.

Resolved, that it is recommended that the property be sold as soon as it can be done on favorable terms.

The recommendation was adopted and E. W. Haile, J. W. Bowen, N. Smith, and J. Barret were appointed a committee to meet with a like group from Enon Association to implement the resolutions.[15]

The friends of Enon College rallied to her support so that within twelve months over half of the debt was paid and the balance was expected to be liquidated promptly. Fisk withdrew his court action and the dark clouds which had hung menacingly over the college seemed at last to be dispersing. At the Salem annual meeting in 1856, the Enon College committee concluded: "Thus the prospect is presented to the Association that this embarrassing difficulty will be speedily adjusted. Your committee congratulate the Association upon the honorable disposition of this aggravated affair." [16]

From 1856 to 1882 the story of Enon College has escaped

---

[14] *Minutes of the Thirty-First Annual Session of the Salem Association of United Baptists, September 16-19, 1854* (McMinnville, Tennessee: The Enterprise Office, 1855) , p. 2.

[15] *Minutes of the Thirty-Second Anniversary of the Salem Baptist Association, September 15-17, 1855* (Lebanon: Herald Office, 1855) , p. 5.

[16] *Minutes of the Thirty-Third Anniversary of the Salem Baptist Association, September 20-22, 1856* (Lebanon: Herald Office, 1856) , p. 4.

recording. Surely the school was closed during most or all of the Civil War years. According to local tradition, Enon College was reopened soon after the war and continued until it failed for lack of financial support in 1882. The records of the Salem Association in that year refer briefly to Enon College as "having failed." It was, in fact, one of three educational institutions drawing partial support from the Salem Association, all of whose failures were recorded during the same year.[17] Records of the final sale and disposition of the college property are thought to have been among the official papers of Trousdale County destroyed when the court house at Hartsville was swept by fire in 1900.

Enon College is nowhere mentioned in the published minutes of the Enon Association of United Baptists for the years 1866-1900, except as the mailing address for the clerk of the association, James L. Carson, in 1869. From time to time minutes of the Enon Association recorded brief recommendations of schools and colleges, but there was nothing said about Enon College. Union University, Hartsville Female Institute, Willette Academy, and Bellewood Institute were recommended as Enon College was ignored.

The Post Office Department had changed the post office name from Wirt College to Enon College March 1, 1854, and appointed Edwin Lindsley Payne postmaster. Department records show that the post office at Enon College was discontinued in 1866 but re-established July 3, 1867, when Robert Eudaley was made postmaster. In 1870, Edwin Lindsley Payne again became postmaster and was succeeded by his son Edwin Sanders Payne July 28, 1873.[18]

The community retained the name of Enon College for several years after the school failed. In 1902, the post office was closed and postal service was extended to the area from nearby Castalian Springs.[19]

---

[17] *Minutes of the Sixtieth Anniversary of the Salem Baptist Association, September 15-16, 1882* (Nashville: Messenger Office, 1882), p. 9.

[18] *United States Postal Records* confuse the Paynes, father Edwin Lindsley and son Edwin Sanders, by mistakenly listing the 1870 appointment to Edward L. and the 1873 appointment to Edward S.

[19] Hartsville *Vidette*, September 10, 1970.

Chapter II

HOWARD FEMALE COLLEGE

HOWARD FEMALE INSTITUTE became the first educational institution in Gallatin authorized to grant degrees when it was established in 1856 by the local Howard Lodge No. 13 of the Independent Order of Odd Fellows. Its origins, however, can be traced back at least three decades to the Gallatin Female Academy where classes, offering the approximate equivalent of today's elementary and high school course work, were being conducted in 1824.[1] The certain date that the female academy first opened its doors to students is not known.

Contemporary newspaper accounts show that during the latter half of 1828, the academy had an enrollment of approximately 80 girls and Charles L. Jeffries was headmaster. He was assisted by a faculty of three teachers—"Mrs. Hunts, Miss Lewis, and Miss Bledsoe"—and three trustees: J. J. White, William Trousdale, and Elijah Boddie.[2]

A charter of incorporation was granted to Gallatin Female Academy on January 18, 1836, by the State Legislature. William P. Rowles[3] was superintendent and a member of the board of trustees which was, in addition, composed of Harris Odom, Oscar F. Bledsoe, Richard May, James A. Blackmore, Daniel Saffarans, A. D. Duval, H. B. Vaughn, Elijah Boddie, William Trousdale, and Josephus Conn Guild.[4]

Within twelve months the trustees announced plans to make

---

[1] Eliza Allen, later to become the first wife of Governor Sam Houston, was a student at the academy in 1824. Walter T. Durham, *Old Sumner, A History of Sumner County, Tennessee, From 1805 to 1861* (Nashville: Parthenon Press, 1972), p. 186.

[2] *National Banner and Nashville Whig*, January 16, 1829. Announcement by Jeffries printed in the Gallatin *Journal*, July 26, 1828, in which reference was made to the opening of the "second session" of the academy on the first Monday of August probably meant that it was the second session of the year—possibly the second session with Jeffries as principal—but surely not the second session in the school's history.

[3] Rowles, during his lifetime, served as an educator, surgeon, preacher, writer, editor, soldier, and businessman.

[4] *Tennessee Acts, 1835-36*, p. 192.

the academy "one of the best schools in the Western country" [5] with funds recently "procured to a large amount." By this time Rowles was no longer at the academy and the board of trustees had been reduced from eleven members to seven with only May, Boddie, and Blackmore retained from the prior group. New members were William Edwards, Thomas A. Baber, Joel Parrish, and J. W. Baldridge. The revamped board of trustees outlined its plans in the Gallatin *Union* of January 20, 1837:

> Suitable buildings for the ensuing year will be rented, and, in the course of the summer, a large, elegant and commodius Academy will be erected. Philosophical apparatus, maps and Globes . . . are already in possession. . . .
>
> The Services of the Rev. John W. Hall, as President, have been procured by the Board; under whom the best teachers in all branches of literature and science will be employed. In a word, the Trustees are determined if money, competent instructors and all the necessary facilities for imparting instruction will avail to make this one of the first institutions in the west. That its location is favorable will be admitted by all who are acquainted with the health, beauty, general intelligence, virtue, and sound morality of the town and county in which it is located.

The trustees' promise to erect a large academy building was fulfilled during 1837 when a permanent two-story brick structure was built on East Main Street on a site purchased from John D. Tomkins for $800. This building, greatly expanded in later years, became the home of Howard Female Institute—later Howard College.[6] The academy building of 1837 was apparently located in the center of a one and one-quarter acre tract made up of town lots numbered 7, 8, 15 and 16, less a thirty foot strip along the eastern boundary adjoining Tomkin's residence. Lots numbered 7 and 8 lay along the south side of East Main Street and lots numbered 15 and 16, at the rear of the first two, faced the north side of Smith Street. These lots are at the center of the property now occupied by Howard Elementary School.[7]

---

[5] Gallatin *Union,* January 20, 1837.

[6] Durham, *ibid.,* p. 316.

[7] *SCR, Deed Book #16,* p. 431.

While the new academy building was under construction, the trustees changed the name of the Gallatin Female Academy to the Sumner Female Academy to which the State Legislature granted a charter during the same year. The school was authorized to issue capital stock in the amount of $75,000, certainly the source of much of the money used in the construction program. For reasons not known, the presidency of John W. Hall was terminated; and in the early summer of 1838, J. B. Blackington became superintendent in his place.[8] Blackington, seemingly under criticism for the rigid discipline that he maintained, left the school in 1839 and was replaced by William H. Marquess, former president of Zanesville Female Academy, Zanesville, Ohio.[9] Marquess remained at the head of the school for three or four years.

The story of the tenure of the Ohio educator as president is cloaked with the same obscurity that surrounds the last years of the Sumner Academy, although it is known that Marquess was followed as president by the Rev. E. McMillan, minister at Shiloh and Gallatin Presbyterian Churches. The academy, like hundreds of private schools of the period, fell upon hard times; and financial distress prompted the trustees to abandon operation of the school in 1855 and to convey the land and building to the prosperous local Howard Lodge No. 13, I.O.O.F., in 1856.[10] Before abandoning their school property to the Howard Lodge, the trustees apparently sought unsuccessfully to induce Marquess to return as president and may have offered the position to a Rev. Mr. Slater.

In fact, the school building and real estate were sold by court order to satisfy creditors in 1855 but were purchased by Charles E. Boddie, acting for the trustees. Boddie then executed a deed conveying the property to the trustees of Sumner Female Institute with provisions that the facility should be used perpetually

---

[8] Durham, *ibid.*, p. 316.

[9] *Ibid.*, p. 318.

[10] "The Lodge was then in a very prosperous condition, owned good property in our town, to wit: A three-story building, located on the square, with two good store rooms in the first; a Town Hall in the second and a good Odd Fellows Hall in the third story." Gallatin *Examiner*, September 29, 1876.

as a school and that the property could not be attached or held for the debts of the school. The names of trustees listed in Boddie's deed were Charles E. Boddie, Josephus C. Guild, H. B. Vaughn, Benjamin F. Allen, William Trousdale, F. A. Sporer, James Alexander, J. N. Head, James J. Turner, and William H. Solomon.[11] The lodge had apparently agreed to sponsor a new school on the property as a charter was granted to Howard Female Institute by the State Legislature, February 18, 1856, with the provision that the school's governing body—a board of visitors—would be elected by Howard Lodge from among its membership. The charter delegated to the president and the board of visitors "full power to confer degrees and grant diplomas usually granted and conferred by first rate female institutions."[12]

Hard upon the heels of the charter came Howard Female Institute's first catalog with the run-on title of *Announcement of the Howard Female Institute, Gallatin, Sumner County, Tennessee, Projected by Howard Lodge No. 13, I.O.O.F., chartered by the Legislature of Tennessee, 1856.*[13] The catalog, circulated in Sumner and surrounding counties, called students to a first "partial session" to be held from the first Monday in April to July 4, 1856. Joseph Smith Fowler, an educator well-known in Middle Tennessee and Southern Kentucky, was chosen to be the first president of the school and F. A. Sporer, a popular local music teacher, was the first faculty member selected. An article in the catalog called attention to Sporer's selection and promised "equal care" in the selection of other faculty members.

Pointing out to prospective students that classes would meet "in the building formerly occupied for a female academy" and recently "presented to the Lodge" the catalog editor explained that, although there were ample accommodations in private homes for boarding students, "The Lodge designs to erect ample additions for an extensive boarding house." An artist's rendering of the building, remodeled and handsomely enlarged, was prominently displayed in the catalog.

[11] *SCR, Deed Book #23*, p. 271.
[12] *Tennessee Acts, 1855-56*, p. 352.
[13] Printed at Nashville by A. A. Stitt.

The board of visitors for Howard Female Institute listed in its first catalog was composed of seven members: President Fowler, T. C. Trimble, B. F. Allen, W. S. Munday, R. T. Bush, William Moore, and Thomas Boyers, all elected by Howard Lodge. The officers of the Grand Lodge, I.O.O.F., of Tennessee were made honorary members of the board.

When Howard Lodge engaged Joseph Smith Fowler to become president of the school, one of its own members was left sorely disappointed that he had been passed over in the selection. W. A. Harrison, Odd Fellow, pastor of the Shiloh and Gallatin Presbyterian Churches, and son-in-law of influential local businessman J. R. A. Tompkins, was bitterly aggrieved. As a lodge member Harrison had helped draw up the charter for the new school and as a Presbyterian minister, whose predecessor had been president of the school, he expected to become its head. Determined to unseat the new president, Harrison seized upon a report, allegedly circulating in Wilson and Rutherford Counties, which suggested that Fowler held unorthodox religious views. The young preacher, who had only three years earlier been graduated from Seminary, interviewed Fowler and concluded that he was an infidel. At once Thomas Boyers, then serving as chairman of the board of visitors, received a visit from Harrison who charged insistently that Fowler was an infidel and thus unworthy of the position that he held. Boyers later convened a meeting of the board of visitors and Harrison restated his accusation against Fowler. In a pamphlet that he later wrote in an attempt to justify his actions, Harrison said that in his interviews with Fowler he discovered that Fowler regarded religion as superstition and the Bible "not inspired." He wrote, "I was shocked at the thought of having a confirmed and inveterate infidel at the head of a *female* school." [14]

The board of visitors, after hearing the charges by Harrison, examined Fowler and addressed a letter to him asking for his reply. Fowler responded at once that he was not then and never had been an infidel. A circular stating that infidel opinions had been imputed to Professor Fowler reproduced the correspondence

---

[14] W. A. Harrison, *Conclusive Proof that Mr. Jo. Smith Fowler, Principal of Gallatin Female Institute is an Infidel* (Nashville: Printed by E. Valette, 1856), p. 8.

that had been exchanged. It was published and circulated by the board.

Correspondence

Gallatin, June 4th, 1856

We, the Visitors of Howard Female Institute, in order to correct certain unfounded reports, which have been circulated in this community, imputing infidel opinions to Prof. Fowler the Principal of said Institute, and thus to affect the character of our School beg leave to call attention to the following correspondence. The order of Odd Fellows, under whose charge said Institute is conducted, while it holds in high respect and reverence the great truths of the Bible and Christianity, it studiously voids all affinity with sects, either religious or political—its motto being universal toleration to all. We trust the mere perusal of the correspondence will be sufficient to disabuse the minds of all who may have been improperly prejudiced by said reports.

> T. C. TRIMBLE
> W. S. MUNDAY
> W.M. MOORE
> T. BOYERS
> B. F. ALLEN

Hon. Jos S. Fowler, Dear Sir: Having learned that reports are now in circulation, in this community, to the effect that you are an infidel, and occupying the position we do, as Visitors to the Institute of which you are Principal, we deem it an act of justice, both to you and ourselves, as well as patrons of the school, to address you this note, simply asking if such reports be correct. Yours very respectfully,

> T. C. TRIMBLE
> W. M. MOORE
> BENJ. F. ALLEN
> T. BOYERS
> WM. S. MUNDAY

Gallatin, June 4th, 1856.

Messrs. T. C. Trimble, Wm. Moore, Benj. F. Allen, Wm. S. Munday, Thos. Boyers: Dear Sirs: Your polite reference to a report now circulating in this community, to the effect that I am an infidel, has just been received.—Your official position as Guardians of the "Howard Female Institute" entitles you to my unequivocal reply. It also affords me pleasure to have an opportunity to correct any improper impressions that have been made upon the minds of the citizens of this or any community, in which this report may have obtained credence. My own relation to yourselves, to the "Institute" and the public, renders it proper that I should reply to your inquiry.

I have, gentlemen, only to say, that, neither at this, nor any former period of my life, have I had any hesitancy in replying at once to such an inquiry. I answer your inquiry in the negative, and thus give an unqualified denial to the truth of such a report. I have ever held that all Scripture is given by the inspiration of God. This, I presume, will satisfy all who are willing that I should have the privilege of stating my position for myself. Fair men, I am fully persuaded, will allow me that right. With sentiments of the highest regard, your obedient servant,

Jos. S. Fowler

With the circulation of Fowler's denial, the board of visitors had taken its last action and considered the case closed. But to Harrison the case was yet open, and he distributed a handbill reiterating his charges against Fowler. When editor Thomas Boyers of the Gallatin *Examiner* suggested in his newspaper that the matter had been discussed enough, Harrison responded by issuing a thirty-one page pamphlet which purported to offer *Conclusive Proof that Mr. Jo. Smith Fowler . . . is an Infidel.*[15]

Despite the confident tenor of the pamphlet's title, Harrison's arguments were weak indeed. Of Fowler he wrote, "He is not an infidel of the Paine or Voltaire kind, but that he is an infidel of the Agassiz and Dewey stamp, his own defense most clearly proves." He recalled his interview with Fowler and his resultant conviction that Fowler was an infidel. Harrison included in the pamphlet testimonial statements made in his own behalf including a lengthy personal endorsement from the aging Judge John J. White of Gallatin.

The only reaction to Harrison's published charges in evidence today is Joseph Smith Fowler's response which was made also in pamphlet form with the title *An Examination of a Scurrilous Pamphlet Under the Vaunting Title "Conclusive Proof that Jo.*

---

15 *Ibid.*

19

Smith Fowler is an Infidel," Written and Circulated by a Certain W. A. Harrison, His Aiders and Abettors. Fowler's rebuttal was printed by Gray and Boyers at the *Examiner* office in Gallatin early in 1857.

Of the two writers, Fowler was decidedly the better pamphleteer; and after the appearance of his answer to Harrison, the issue seems to have been dropped. The public apparently agreed with Fowler that Harrison's attack on him had been motivated by jealousy arising from Harrison's failure to be selected president of the new institute. Both men continued to live in Gallatin, the clergyman Harrison until 1859 and the educator Fowler until 1861.[16]

Early in 1858, friends of Howard Female Institute decided that the school was entitled to a share of the Sumner County allotment of the state academy fund, all of which at that time was being directed to Transmontania Academy at Gallatin. A private act was consequently offered and passed by the Legislature January 25, 1858, authorizing the State of Tennessee to divide the academy fund in Sumner County between Howard and Transmontania, share and share alike.[17] Less than six weeks later, however, the "sharing" act was repealed and the total fund restored to Transmontania Academy.[18]

The *Catalog of the Officers and Pupils of Howard Female Institute For the Year 1858* [19] listed 131 "undergraduates" from the previous year with ten in the graduating class of '58. All of the seniors had home addresses in Sumner County while a few of the other students were from homes outside of the county. Boarding was available in Gallatin private homes at the rate of $50 for a term of five months. Members of the board of visitors for 1858 were President Fowler, Thomas C. Trimble, Thomas Boyers, William Moore, Benjamin F. Allen, W. S. Munday, and George W. Winchester. The names of the officers of the state Grand

---

[16] Durham, *ibid.*, p. 455.

[17] *Tennessee Acts, 1857-58*, p. 48.

[18] *Ibid.*, p. 262.

[19] Copy at Tennessee State Library and Archives, Nashville. Printed at Gallatin by Gray and Boyers, 1858.

Lodge, I.O.O.F., again appeared as honorary members of the board of visitors.

The first student news and literary publication, *The Bud of Thought,* appeared in 1860, "edited by the young ladies of Howard Female Institute" and printed at Gallatin by John S. Ward.[20] The first issue was introduced with the promise that it would be published weekly by the senior class but subsequent issues, if any, seem to have escaped preservation.

The prevailing political view of *The Bud of Thought* was pro-union and anti-secession. A visit to the school by former Governor Foote of Mississippi during which he spoke in support of preserving the Union and against secession was endorsed and reported fully. An editorial bearing the heading "America and our Union Forever" proclaimed the young writer's disdain for withdrawal or secession. While this enthusiastic Unionist sentiment coincided with the political convictions of the school's president, it also reflected a sentiment still strongly held in Sumner County at that time. It had been less than thirty years since Andrew Jackson had issued the dramatic challenge: "Our federal union—it must be preserved." And most Sumner Countians were loath to turn their backs on Old Hickory.

The Bud of Thought listed members of the board of visitors for 1860: President Fowler, William Moore, W. S. Munday, B. F. Allen, Thomas C. Douglass, C. E. Boddie, and W. B. Bate. In addition to the president, the names of four faculty members were mentioned: F. A. Sporer, professor of music; Miss Willie Wilber, teacher of art and French; Miss Eliza McCracken, teacher of natural science and assistant in mathematics; and Miss Maggie D. Boxley, governess and teacher of English literature.

With secession and the outbreak of the Civil War in 1861, Howard Female Institute closed its doors. President Fowler, strongly sympathetic with the Union, made his way to Springfield, Illinois. He would return to Tennessee the next year to serve as state comptroller under Governor Andrew Johnson and later, from 1866-1871, to serve as one of Tennessee's two United States

---

[20] Copy at Edward Ward Carmack Public Library, Gallatin.

Senators. He would be one of seven Republican senators to vote against the impeachment of President Andrew Johnson! [21]

During the war years the Howard Female Institute property and building were frequently used by Federal troops occupying the Gallatin area. A memorandum written ten years later described the use made of the property:

> They [Federal troops] took possession of our Lodge and school buildings and property, and destroyed everything, both our school and Lodge property and fixtures of every kind. Our Lodge and school were well-furnished with first-class furniture and fixtures of every kind, all of which the armies made a perfect wreck and used our Lodge and school buildings during the war for hospital and other purposes, and when the war closed our buildings were a complete wreck.[22]

The end of the war marked a new beginning for Howard Female Institute. The members of Howard Lodge, facing pre-war debts and the threat of a sheriff's sale of the college's war-wrecked facilities, turned to the national Grand Lodge for financial assistance. While the Grand Lodge had no funds available to assist Howard Female Institute, permission was granted Howard Lodge to solicit aid from the various lodges in the United States.

Professor Hugh Blair Todd, a native of Fredericksburg, Virginia, "a fine teacher and scholar and a zealous and emphatic Odd Fellow," was elected president of Howard Female Institute and assigned the task of raising funds sufficient to re-activate the school. "Prof. Todd started on his mission for aid and met with good success. The lodges in many of the states contributed very liberally. . . . Todd succeeded in obtaining means sufficient to repair and refit the Institute for school purposes again." [23] When the new president had obtained subscriptions amounting to approximately $12,000, Howard Female Institute, closed for five years, reopened for instruction in April, 1866.[24]

Todd set about rehabilitating the war-wrecked campus with

---

[21] *Biographical Directory of the American Congress, 1774-1949* (Washington, D.C.: U.S. Government Printing Office, 1950), p. 178.

[22] Gallatin *Examiner,* September 29, 1876.

[23] *Ibid.*

[24] Summer County *News,* August 13, 1931.

vigor. The buildings were put in good condition and the green areas were planted with flowers and trees.

While young boys were accepted for the lower grades, Howard was still pre-eminently a girls school. The young ladies wore uniform dresses—in the summer white with blue aprons and a white leghorn hat with blue ribbon. On public occasions they marched to and from school in unbroken ranks as, according to Todd's daughter, "Punishment swift and dire befell anyone who missed step or broke ranks." The president's "method of punishment was a vigorous shake which sent hairpins flying and was so salutary that the offense was not often repeated." [25]

In spite of his energy and dedication, Todd found operating the institute was a very trying task in the postwar years during which he served it. While school had opened in 1866 with an enrollment of 272,[26] the number of students steadily declined during the next six years. The size of his graduating classes dropped regularly from sixteen members in 1867 to five in 1870.[27]

The loss of enrollment had further reduced revenues and Todd experienced considerable difficulty in obtaining capable teachers for his faculty. When Miss Sue Wynne, daughter of Col. A. R. Wynne of Castalian Springs, declined to join the faculty in 1869, Todd explained to her that his offer to pay her $125 per session of five months was $25 more than he had paid any other woman on the staff. Pleading for her to reconsider, Todd set forth the straitened condition of his finances in a letter preserved in the *George W. Wynne Papers.*

> At least one third of my pupils are from families unable to pay anything and from whom I never expect one dollar. And those of Gallatin and Sumner County who do pay are very slow about it. . . . Since this session began, I have received but 45 dollars from Gallatin and this county and have had to borrow money to pay my teachers. . . .

By the end of the year 1871 Todd had decided to resign as head of the school and to give up the lease that he held on its

---

[25] *Ibid.*
[26] *Ibid.*
[27] *Ibid.,* March 9, 1961.

property. The specific circumstances that prompted his resignation are not known although the financial difficulties faced by the school and its patrons were reasons enough. Todd inserted the following letter in the Gallatin *Examiner* January 26, 1872:

To the Patrons and Friends of Howard Female College.

Though my lease on College Buildings, furniture and grounds, does not terminate for some twenty months yet, and though the school over which it is my honor to preside is unusually large, numbering considerably over one-hundred pupils, during the winter months, when schools of the kind are usually much smaller —still, I have it a duty which I owe to myself and others to relinquish to the Lodge, from which I obtained it, my lease, and, to resign my position as Principal of Howard Female College, to take effect with close of present session ending with January.

I shall ever hold, in grateful recollection, those who have continued to honor me with their patronage and who have been true in their friendship, and shall often ask upon them, the blessings of Him, who is too wise and good to err.

Mine has been truly a responsible, and, under the circumstances surrounding me and the Institution, a very trying position, I feel that in the love of those under my charge, and in the fear of God, I have been faithful to the high and important trusts committed to my keeping.

On many accounts it will be painful to leave Gallatin as a home and to break off associations with so many long tried and true friends,—I have sought to be an active instrument of good to all, of injury to none, and have labored hard to render my poor services a blessing to the town and county.

If my patrons and friends and the community generally, will meet me on coming Thursday evening 23rd, at half past six o'clock, in the Christian Church, I will try to make them a pleasant little talk, and will, as I feel it due them and myself, give some reasons for the course I have thought it best to pursue.

H. B. TODD

Todd's resignation must have been a surprise to the board of visitors. The same issue of the Gallatin newspaper that printed his letter of resignation also published notice from the secretary of the board that the school was actively seeking applications from candidates who would replace Todd. In its news column the *Examiner* listed the names of the board of visitors, newly elected by Howard Lodge, for the year 1872: W. F. Holder, R. C. Parker, H. B. Vaughn, James House, John T. Baber, and James G. Vaughn, secretary and treasurer.[28]

From among the applicants to replace Todd, the new board of visitors selected Professor A. J. Wood, a respected local teacher, as principal. Todd's daughter remembered Wood as "a capable and popular teacher, supported by good patronage." [29] He served as principal of Howard Female Institute until 1874. Sometime thereafter he became president of the Gallatin Male Academy, a position in which he was identified by the Gallatin *Examiner,* August 14, 1880.

Wood's years at Howard were followed by a four year period during which John M. Walton operated his Neophogen Male and Female College in the facilities that had housed Howard Female Institute since its beginnings. The Walton interlude is detailed at length in the chapter entitled Neophogen Male and Female College.

As financial woes pointed to the closing of Neophogen College, Howard Lodge's board of visitors announced that Howard Female Institute would be reopened September 2, 1878, and that they had elected the Rev. W. H. Haynes president.[30] The Howard announcement was made over the signature of John T. Baber, secretary of the board. His notice contained the succinct admonition to patrons: "No boys however small admitted." Walton's co-educational experiment would not be continued at Howard Female Institute! [31]

The use of the name Howard Female *College* apparently first occurred during Todd's administration and was used interchangeably with Howard Female Institute thereafter. "Howard Female College Closing Exercises" was a headline in the Gallatin *Examiner* June 11, 1879, under which was told the story of a commencement observation that occupied three consecutive

---

[28] Gallatin *Examiner,* January 20, 1872.

[29] Sumner County *News,* August 13, 1931.

[30] Gallatin *Examiner,* January 25, 1878. A year earlier Haynes had opened a female school in Gallatin known as Haynes' Seminary for Young Ladies. *Ibid.,* August 3, 1877.

[31] *Ibid.,* January 25, 1878.

nights. This was the close of the first year of Haynes' administration and local attention was focused on the events at the college. The newspaper account stated, "Our citizens have manifested great interest in these exercises, numbers being unable to obtain seats or even standing room in the hall of the College. The patrons of the school express themselves as well satisfied with Professor Haynes' management. His efficient corps of assistants are also deserving of much praise for the conscientious manner in which they have discharged their duties to their pupils." The "exercises" consisted of vocal and instrumental music, speeches, dialogues, and recitations of various types.

The school continued with Professor Haynes as president for three years. Then, at the end of the school year 1881-82, Haynes was succeeded in the presidency by A. M. Burney, a veteran educator and late newspaper editor at McMinnville who, before he left Howard, would serve the longest tenure in that office of anyone in the school's history.[32]

During Burney's years the school further developed its music program. Musical events were staged frequently during the school year. One such "Musical Recitation" was held in the College Chapel of Howard Female College December 8, 1884, at 6:30 p.m. The printed "Programme" listed Miss E. F. Rider as Director and the following pupils as performers of musical numbers: Lena Neelly, Mattie B. Bass, Alice Williamson, Pollie Barr, Mary Martin, Lizzie Brown, Alice Brown, Mamie Gloster, Louise Allen, Kittie Pickering, Allie Shivers, Virgie Dorris, Vena Stuart, Willie Stuart, Tennie Woodson, Virgie Woodson, Eliza Reid, Jennie

---

[32] Burney was born in Maury County, Tennessee, June 4, 1833. At the age of 23 he became president of McCain's Academy and nine years later in 1865 he was elected president of Mooresville Academy. In 1869 he accepted the presidency of Robert Donnell Institute and in 1871 he became president of Cumberland Female College at McMinnville. While still at McMinnville in 1880 he became a partner in a weekly newspaper, the *Southern Standard,* and soon thereafter became sole owner and publisher. He suspended publication in 1882 and removed to Gallatin to become president of Howard Female College. Burney seems to have been a well-known figure throughout the state as is indicated by his election in 1873 as Grand Master of the statewide Independent Order of Odd Fellows. He died April 19, 1895. A memorial to Burney in the form of a stone tablet containing most of this information was placed within the walls of the main building of Howard College a few months after his death. The tablet is now the property of Mr. and Mrs. Jack Allindre, Rock Bridge Community, Sumner County.

Shafer, Willie Patterson, M. Gillenwater, S. Dorris, and Hattie Cartwright.[33]

In an invitation mailed to patrons of Howard Female College in 1885, Miss Rider listed the student performers in a "Programme" to be offered March 9, 1885. They were Misses Annie Chenault, Alice Turner, Mary Purdy, Celia Walton, Fannie and Thankful Barry, John Davis, Annie Dorris, Emma Joyner, Eva Brown, Maybelle Andrews, Lizzie Saunders, Ella and Lula Lewis, Bessie Schell, Annie Seay, Jennie Shafer, Minnie Brown, Willie Staly, and Maria Reid.[34]

A news sheet called the *Howard College Argus,* dated June 4, 1885, "devoted to the interests of Howard Female College" and "edited by the faculty," outlined the commencement program that was concluded on that same date. The *Argus,* if judged by this single issue, was a promotional sheet for the college. It contained statements of policy for the school's operation and set forth a variety of information calculated to interest parents in sending their daughters to Howard College.

The *Argus* emphasized the school's determined non-denominational policy which had been initiated when Howard Lodge had become its owner and sponsor. "The fact that Howard Female College is not a denominational school and not run in the interest of any church nor intended to build up church enterprises, but is a literary institution standing upon its own merits, will not fail to attract the attention of thoughtful fathers and mothers," the *Argus* said. "Besides this liberal toleration in religious matters is a Christian duty as well as a refined accomplishment, and this can be best taught and practiced where all are recognized as on equality in matters of faith and conscience. This is precisely the kind of association we have here in school."

In separate notices the *Argus* pointed out that boarding charges for a five month term were $80, that boarding students received special instruction in "social culture and refinement of manners," and that the music teacher Miss Rider had declined a position on the faculty of a conservatory in Illinois to stay at Howard. It was

[33] Kenneth Thomson Private Collection.
[34] *Ibid.*

27

further noted that "the course of study in this school is thoroughly English," that the departments of art and music were "of high order" and "abreast of the times," and that the next session of school would begin on the first Monday in September, 1885.

In a strong statement doubtless drawn by President Burney, the *Argus* praised the intellectual accomplishments attained by Howard students: "Those who desire their daughters educated in solid intellectual requirements and in the accomplishments that are both graceful and useful with the polish of manners and morals, will find Howard Female College a place peculiarly suited to that purpose. Those who desire a mere outside show, without the reality, will do well to go elsewhere for it. There are schools that will engage to put on a thin finish, through which ignorance and rudeness show their deformity in all after life, but this is not one of that number. Mind is made the basis of all culture here and intellectual accomplishments are the result."

A sign that remodeling and new construction was being planned at Howard was indicated in the *Argus* commencement announcement of 1885. A cantata was held at the Opera House[35] "for the benefit of the fund for improving the college edifice and erecting the new wing." That the cantata and perhaps other efforts to raise funds had not been very productive was suggested by an editorial query directed to the merchants of Gallatin by the *Examiner,* September 12, 1885: "Are the merchants and furnishers of Gallatin willing to stand still and see Howard College checked in her rapid and steady growth for want of room to hold her boarders? Will they stand and croak hard times while they check their own prosperity?"

There was apparently enough money raised by public subscription to enable construction to begin on a major addition to the main building. The new wing was to be primarily devoted to providing dormitory space for the increasing number of boarding students. Before the new construction was completed, however, the scanty funds had been exhausted. With no other monies forthcoming from Howard Lodge or from the community at

[35] Located upstairs over the present Clark Drug Store on East Main Street in Gallatin.

large, A. M. Burney, drawing on his own personal funds, in September, 1886, offered to "advance one thousand dollars for the purpose of completing the work now in progress on the new wing of Howard Female College for and in consideration of the fact that you extend the term of my present lease on the College premises and include the new wing for a period of five years from the expiration of the same on the same terms and conditions therein stated." [36] Burney's offer was accepted by the board of visitors and ratified by Howard Lodge.[37] The building was completed sometime in late 1886 or early 1887 so that the board of visitors could report to the lodge June 30, 1887, that "our buildings and grounds are in fine condition and the school in a flourishing condition under the wise management of Prof. A. M. Burney." [38]

The commencement exercises at Howard Female College in 1887 were recognized as the fiftieth such graduation on the Howard East Main Street campus. The fifty commencements must have included those of the Gallatin Female Academy in the early 1830's to compensate for the years lost during the Civil War as well as those of the Sumner Female Academy prior to the formation of Howard Female Institute. A newspaper account of the commencement exercises referred to the "celebration of the fiftieth commencement by the meeting of all the *alumnae* for the fifty years of the school, and the historical sketch of the institution under the fifteen presidents up to the present, By Col. Thos. Boyers." [39] The newspaper's use of the term *alumnae* suggests that only coeds from the Neophogen years were invited or that former Neophogen students were excluded altogether. On the other hand, Howard Lodge seemed always to claim that Neophgen College was its institution and to regard it as Howard College operating temporarily under another name. The few

[36] *Minutes of Howard Lodge No. 13, I.O.O.F., Minute Book 1885-1905*, p. 52. John Garrott Private Collection. (Cited hereafter as *Howard Minute Book, 1885-1905*).

[37] *Ibid.*

[38] *Ibid.*, p. 67.

[39] Clipping from Gallatin *Examiner*, June, 1887. Exact date not indicated. Boyers' speech was not reported nor otherwise preserved.

boys who attended Howard did so at an early age and were not permitted to remain in school during their upper grade years. Hence, there had been male students but no alumni.

The fiftieth anniversary commencement was addressed by Tennessee Governor Robert L. Taylor. The valedictory address was made by Kate Thomson of Delki, Louisiana, and the salutatory address by Vena Stuart of Gallatin who later became a beloved public school teacher.[40] Members of the graduating class in "the regular literary course" were, in addition to Misses Thomson and Stuart, Maggie Glasgow, Louise Allen, Ada Head, and Lillie Henley of Gallatin; Vallie Hibbett, Laura Youree, Willie Stuart, and Celia Walton of Sumner County; Laura Morris, Monroe, Louisiana; Sallie Head, Trenton, Louisiana; Carrie Hite, Mexico, Missouri; and Florence Williamson, Culleoka, Tennessee.[41]

In 1888, Burney forged ahead with plans further to improve the facilities of Howard Female College. This time he sought to install a steam heating system but again found the Lodge without the necessary funds to finance the improvement. Instead of borrowing money from Burney as they had done two years earlier, the Lodge and its board of visitors entered into an agreement with him to permit him to install the heating system at his own expense. Burney was to retain ownership of the system with the right to dismantle and remove it if he should so desire. The consideration of the agreement was "that the said apparatus will improve and make the buildings more comfortable and less expensive to the board in keeping up grates and stoves . . . and less expensive to the leasee in the way of fuel and labor." [42] The members of the board of visitors in 1888 were Burney, J. W. Blackmore, S. F. Wilson, A. J. Swaney, W. H. Brown, E. O. Buchanan, and G. N. Guthrie.[43]

The minutes of Howard Lodge show that the membership, at a meeting December 3, 1888, voted to conduct a drive to raise a

---

[40] Vena Stuart Elementary School at Gallatin bears her name. She taught for fifty years in Gallatin before retirement.

[41] Clipping, *ibid.*

[42] *Howard Minute Book, 1885-1905,* pp. 96-97.

[43] *Ibid.*

"Fund for Howard College." [44] No details of the drive are contained in the brief minutes. However, the minutes of a meeting March 25, 1889, suggest that the fund was being raised—at least in part—by selling scholarships to other I.O.O.F. lodges: "A communication from Banner Lodge No. 147 I.O.O.F. of Memphis donating to Howard Lodge No. 13 I.O.O.F. Scholarship No. 10 which had been purchased from Howard College Building fund." [45]

The members of the board of visitors for 1890 were President Burney, A. J. Swaney, S. F. Wilson, James W. Blackmore, E. O. Buchanan, W. C. Blue, and W. H. Brown.[46] The same men were re-elected to serve in 1891.[47]

The loan advanced by Burney to finish the building project in 1886 seems to have amounted to approximately $2,000. The balance due, after reductions, in 1889 was $1,425.80.[48] By 1891, the balance owed was $1,127.14,[49] and in 1892 was $924.64.[50]

Burney's tenure at Howard College continued into the decade of the 1890's. The faculty listing in the catalog for 1890-91 showed Burney as president and proprietor: Boarding Department, Mrs. Burney, superintendent; Mademoiselle L. M. Wuille, governess; Department of Aesthetics, Mademoiselle Wuille, principal; Collegiate Department: A. M. Burney, Miss Tennie Pinkerton, Miss Sallie R. McLean, Miss Lula D. Barton, and Mademoiselle Wuille; Department of Music, Miss Hattie M. Fay and Miss Prudie Simpson; Department of Art, Miss Maggie W. Gunn; and Business Department, Miss Lula D. Barton.[51] Emphasis on the non-sectarian nature of the school was continued: "The Bible is read daily without comment; pupils are encouraged to attend the church of their choice, and free toleration is extended to all creeds, and faith, and exclusive privilege to none." [52] In this

[44] *Ibid.*, p. 101.
[45] *Ibid.*, p. 105.
[46] *Ibid.*, p. 119.
[47] *Ibid.*, p. 140.
[48] *Ibid.*, p. 109.
[49] *Ibid.*, p. 160.
[50] *Ibid.*, p. 182.
[51] *Fifty-Fourth Annual Announcement of Howard Female College, Gallatin, Tennessee, 1890-91* (Nashville: James T. Camp, printer, 1890).
[52] *Ibid.*

31

period approximately one half of the members of the graduating classes were Gallatin students with the others from out of town.[53] Included in the catalog was a letter from the secretary of the Grand Lodge of Tennessee endorsing the school and praising Howard Lodge for its support of it. The letter was careful, however, to point out that the College "is conducted as a private enterprise by Prof. Burney, one of the best educators in the state." [54]

A news story of this century quoting from the catalog of 1891-92 strongly indicates that the "gay nineties" at Howard College were also the "formal nineties":

> The Department of Aesthetics has been added to the college and made distinct and separate from the other departments in order to develop the physical powers, and add polish and grace to the personal appearance of all our boarders, while we train the intellect to grapple with the arts and sciences. All awkward movements of body, discordant tones of voice, and slang words must be abandoned while in this literary home.
>
> The laws of health, attention to personal habits, correct manners, elegant expression and refined tastes will be daily taught and earnestly enforced in the Home Department of our school.
>
> The girls are in daily association with teachers and proprietors, and never leave the premises except in company with one of them. No attention from young men is allowed, except from brothers, and no visits received from any outside of the family except in the presence of a teacher. No promiscuous association with day pupils.[55]

In October, 1891, Howard Lodge offered to permit the Grand Lodge of Tennessee to "assume" Howard Female College "in name, and general claim and supervision" while reserving to itself ownership of the school property and assuming "all financial obligations for teachers and property of the same." [56] Howard Lodge explained its offer in a memorial to the Grand Lodge adopted October 15, 1891:

> To the R W Grand Lodge I.O.O.F. of Tennessee:
> Howard Lodge No. 13. I.O.O.F. under your Jurisdiction would

[53] *Ibid.*
[54] *Ibid.*
[55] Sumner County *News*, March 9, 1961.
[56] *Howard Minute Book, 1885-1905*, pp. 179-181.

respectfully and fraternally represent to your worthy grand body, that we have established, sustained and fostered for thirty-five years past an institution of learning in Gallatin, Tenn., known as Howard Female College, which to-day is in a flourishing condition, and ranks as a first class Female College. Said institution is out of debt, self-sustaining and doing a great work for our beloved order and the public generally.

We believe it would be for the good of our beloved order in the prosecution of its Heaven chosen mission as well as for the country at large to extend the field of its operations and enlarge its sphere of usefulness.

Therefore we propose to your grand body that we will continue to furnish the buildings, premises, and equipments, own and control the property of the college as we have done heretofore for more than one-third of a century and meet all financial obligations for teachers and property of the same, and give you the school in name, and general claim and supervision to be known as Howard Female College, Gallatin, Tenn., the Odd Fellows College for Young Ladies, conducted under the auspices of the Grand Lodge, I.O.O.F. Tennessee. Under this arrangement you are to claim and recognize the school as yours, appoint visitors and lecturers, solicit patronage and enjoy the honor of having a first class college for the education of the orphans and daughters of Odd Fellows throughout the country, and you are to direct and request each subordinate lodge under your jurisdiction to appoint a soliciting agent whose duty it shall be to circulate catalogues and information, and solicit pupils from the brotherhood and the public in general. Said agents are to receive such compensation for their services as may be agreed upon by themselves and the proprietors of the school.

It is herein respectfully suggested that the District Deputy Grand Masters of the State be made by appointment or ex-officio, said agents.

It is not intended to confine said agents to the brotherhood, but they should canvass their sections for pupils and patronage from their neighbors and friends outside of the order and furnish the names and addresses of interested parties to the President of the College that he may correspond with all parties interested in the education of their daughters.

By this means great good may result to the school and also to the order at large in their winning the favor and friendship of good men who may become members of the order and besides all this, it will give the Grand Lodge something to labor for and build up on and nucleus and rallying point around which the order in your Jurisdiction could rally its forces in the great mission of educating the orphan as well as strengthen itself by educating the daughters of Odd Fellows and others, conciliate woman and win her to the order in its work.

Such a step and such an enterprise so congenial and so appropriate would in a few years give the order in this Jurisdiction a commanding attitude that would fire our depleted ranks and make our mission a labor of love as well as be the means of adding to our membership and usefulness.

Let the essential parts of the catalogue be published in your minutes for information to the Lodges of such action on your part as you may deem proper to take.

Arguments Abbreviated

1st The proposition does not require the Grand Lodge to assume any financial responsibility whatever.

2nd It would enlarge the sphere and usefulness of both the School and the order in your Jurisdiction.

3rd It will give our order a prestige and a power over the world that it never had before in this country and thus increase its membership and efficiency.

4th Gallatin is located in the central part of the state and is one of the wealthiest and most accessible places in Tennessee.

5th The Grand Lodge of Tennessee without incurring one cent of expense under this proposition can establish—rather assume as her's one of the best female schools in Tennessee by simply accepting this offer.

This offer read in open Lodge at the stated meeting of Howard Lodge No. 13, I.O.O.F., Monday night Oct 19th 1891, and fully endorsed ratified and made the deed and act of said Lodge.

Witness the signatures of the officers and seal of the Lodge.

This Oct 19th 1891.[57]

A week later Howard's offer was accepted by the Grand Lodge of Tennessee. Howard Female College would enjoy the advantages of the moral support and state-wide promotion available through member lodges of I.O.O.F. However, the agreement with the Grand Lodge specifically eliminated the assistance that Howard College needed most: financial aid.[58]

In a report to Howard Lodge dated July 4, 1892, Burney de-

---

[57] *Ibid.*

[58] *Ibid.,* p. 182.

scribed the state of the college at midyear. He regarded "the progress of pupils in attendance, scholarship, and deportment" as showing "a degree of excellence unsurpassed in this or any other institution." Employing the superlatives that were prominent in the vocabularies of school administrators of the period, Burney declared:

> For the preservation of that most precious of all legacies to young ladies—character, the report for not only this, but all the ten years past stands without a parallel in the history of literary institutions of our country.
>
> For the present and past condition of the property for ten years past, I invite your personal inspection.
>
> Where dirt, dinginess and decay reigned in doors and out ten years ago, now neatness, paint, carpets, papered walls, and polished surfaces meet the eye everywhere. Instead of rusty, broken stoves, a new steam apparatus gently and pleasantly warms all the rooms. Instead of hauling water as was necessary then, we have the best bored well in Gallatin, and a fine cistern and new tank, supplying all the rooms, but I ask your inspection.
>
> Respectfully Submitted
A. M. BURNEY
Lessee[59]

Members of Burney's faculty at this time were Mrs. A. M. Burney, Mademoiselle Wuille, Miss Agnes Orr, Miss Sallie R. McLean, Miss Lillian Crockett, Miss Kate Anderson, Miss Maggie Gunn, Miss Georgia Blair, Miss Sallie Goodloe, and Miss Emma Myers.[60] The members of the board of visitors for 1892 were Burney, S. F. Wilson, Dr. A. J. Swaney, W. C. Blue, J. W. Blackmore, F. F. Pierce, and S. R. Lewis.[61]

The catalog for 1892-1893 was the first issued by Howard College since the informal relationship with the Grand Lodge was established in late 1891 and it took due note of the new arrangement. "Howard College is conducted under the auspices of the Grand Lodge I.O.O.F. of Tennessee. . . . The only object the

---

[59] *Ibid.*, p. 222.

[60] Gallatin *Tennessean,* June 4, 1892.

[61] *Fifty-Sixth Annual Announcement of Howard Female College, Gallatin, Tennessee, 1892-1893* (Nashville: James T. Camp, printer, 1892).

35

Order has in view is to foster and sustain the school." Mention was made that President Burney was a past Grand Master of the Grand Lodge of Tennessee, a fact that undoubtedly was weighed duly when the Grand Lodge decided to identify with Howard College. A strong recommendation under the heading "The I.O.O.F. College" was written and signed by William Austin Smith, Grand Master, and J. R. Harwell, Secretary, the Grand Lodge of Tennessee. They concluded, "It is a school of high standing, and we cheerfully commend it to the patronage of all Odd Fellows and others who have daughters and wards to be educated." [62]

Prospective students reviewing the catalog found listing of the members of the graduating classes for the years 1884 through 1892 and the information that the college awarded two degrees: Mistress of English Literature, M.E., or Mistress of Arts, M.A. They were also confronted with this stern warning found in the section headed *Correspondence:* "Promiscuous correspondence will not be allowed." [63]

The annual report of the board of visitors filed July 5, 1893, and incorporated into the minutes of Howard Lodge, was highly complimentary of President Burney and his operation of the school. Dr. A. J. Swaney and George Boddie made the report for the board and recalled Burney's years at Howard Female College:

> Eleven years ago when the property was leased to the present proprietor it was in a deplorable state of repairs inside and out-side. It was scarcely habitable, much less suitable for a boarding house for young ladies. The Board then used all the rents to pay insurance and make repairs for the first four years, and by economy put the buildings and premises in a passable state of repairs. At the end of this period the Board decided to erect the "East Wing," and took a subscription for the purpose, which proved insufficient, and when the walls were up and the roof on, the carpenters and contractors stopped work, and the building stood unfinished for a few weeks with no work going on. In order to finish the structure and save what had been invested, the Board consumated a trade

[62] *Ibid.*
[63] *Ibid.*

with the Lessee and proprietor to furnish the money, $1,000.00 as an advancement on rents, in consideration for which they extended his lease to the former lease then current, with the understanding mutually that they would not raise the rents during said extension of said lease for a term of five years, and that he would not charge interest on the money advanced by him. After this the Lessee at the request of the Board of Visitors, paid about $600.00.

On the 4th day of July of each year since that date (as well as before) there has been a fair and complete settlement between the Board and Lessee, which are on record in your Minute Book, showing the amount of rent over and above the insurance and necessary repairs each year, has been applied to the liquidation of this money advanced by the lessee. In these annual settlements each year, since advancing the $1,500.00 to complete the building from $50 to $75 has been paid out by the Lessee for valuable improvements to the property for which he has made no charge against the Board. His books show that he has given free tuition alone to worthy orphans and other persons, such as ministers of various denominations, to the sum of $4,875.00 in the eleven years of his administration. The names, dates and amounts of these can be produced and examined by the Lodge or any friend of the School. We think we do not hazard much in saying that this is more than all the educational efforts together have done in the county for this length of time. We think it but just that the facts should be known to you as the management of the school in regard to its finances has been called into question. During all these years the school has flourished and increased in prosperity and popularity beyond anything in its history before. We come now to report upon the last scholastic year, beginning where our report left off one year ago.

Our report shows we were then owing the Lessee

Balance due on Settlement	$ 924.64
He has since paid on pavement	102.00
Insurance on building to T. F. Witherspoon	15.00
Painting on College Roof	42.00
Painting on Chimneys	6.00
Insurance on building D. B. Anderson	58.50
Combination Medal	12.00
	$1,160.14
Credit by Annual Rent	300.00
Balance due Lessee	860.14

We find also that the Lessee has made improvements to the building for which he has made no charge to the amount of $89.50, the same being donated to the College.

The amount of insurance at the present time is as follows, viz:

D. B. Anderson, Agt on three policies $7,300.00
T. F. Witherspoon, Agt carries 1,875.00
Whole Amount of Insurance $9,175.00

The rate of insurance on the building has been reduced from $1.25 to 80 cents in consideration of the reduction of risk occasioned by the building being heated by steam. This reduction has been made since the steam aparatus was put in. The expenses for next year will be much less, as we will have no pavement to build, no roof to paint, etc. The buildings and grounds are in first class condition. The premises are clean, and are an ornament to the town.

The late closing exercises of the College were of the highest order of merit and culture, and received the cordial approval and commendation from the large and appreciative audiences who attended them. The visitors and patrons from a distance went away highly pleased, and were loud in their praise of the management of the school.

GEO. W. BODDIE)
A. J. SWANEY) Committee[64]

In a local newspaper announcement of the opening of the school year 1893-94, President Burney offered free tuition "to worthy orphans and minister's daughters of all denominations." He suggested that each church in the county might select "one worthy orphan for free tuition." [65]

Howard Lodge elected a new board of visitors for the college January 1, 1894. The members were President Burney, F. F. Pierce, J. B. Howison, S. F. Wilson, George A. Seay, J. W. Blackmore, and A. J. Swaney.[66] Later in the year Howard Lodge voted to attach its seal to the diplomas awarded to the graduating class of Howard College and May 29 the lodge decided to attend Howard College commencement services in a body.[67] The board of visitors were instructed by the lodge to amend the school's

---

[64] *Howard Minute Book, 1885-1905*, pp. 257-259.
[65] Gallatin *Tennessean*, September 2, 1893.
[66] *Howard Minute Book, 1885-1905*, p. 277.
[67] *Ibid.*, pp. 292-293.

charter to reflect its accepted name—Howard Female *College*—instead of Howard Female *Institute*.[68] The board reported that the lodge's debt to A. M. Burney had been reduced to an outstanding amount of $663.89 and that the school was "well conducted and the property is well cared for and in a good state of repair."[69]

The most successful period in Howard College's history came to an unexpected end in the spring of 1895 with the death of President Burney. In the autumn school opened as usual, but the strong leadership of the late president was sorely missed.

Most of the events in the life of Howard Female College from 1895 until 1902 seem to have escaped recording. The minutes of the lodge are recorded during this period but are silent about Howard College. Later newspaper histories of the school claim that a man named "Hubbard" followed Burney as president, but no further information is supplied.[70]

In 1897, A. C. Bigger, characterized as "a young man of energy and ability"[71] became president of the college. It was recalled that he "had a splendid, cooperative faculty, a firm and kind discipline . . . and the school prospered under his guidance."[72] It is known that Bigger's administration continued at least into the autumn of 1899,[73] and that Z. K. Griffin succeeded him as president of Howard College in 1900 and served at least into the year 1905.[74]

In September, 1901, the members of Griffin's faculty were listed in a Gallatin newspaper: Misses Jennie Williams, Tommie Bell Chambers, Amy Reynolds, Lena Stringer, Mattie Martin, Sallie Caruthers, and Mrs. Prudence Simpson Dresser.[75]

Howard Lodge elected the members of its board of visitors in early 1902: W. F. Albright, A. J. Swaney, J. T. Baskerville, G. W.

[68] *Ibid.*, p. 298.
[69] *Ibid.*, p. 299.
[70] Sumner County *News*, April 1, 1909.
[71] *Ibid.*, August 13, 1931.
[72] *Ibid.*
[73] Gallatin *Semi-Weekly News*, October 14, 1899.
[74] *Howard Minute Book, 1885-1905*, pp. 309, 404. Also Sumner County *News*, August 13, 1931.
[75] Gallatin *Examiner*, September 7, 1901.

Boddie, P. L. Anderson, and J. W. Blackmore.[76] Later in the year the Lodge voted to send a memorial to the United States Congress seeking financial restitution for damages to the school property when in the use of Federal troops during the Civil War.[77] The relief sought was never granted.

The board of visitors elected for 1903 was composed of J. W. Blackmore, Dr. A. J. Swaney, J. T. Baskerville, G. W. Boddie, W. F. Albright, and P. L. Anderson.[78] When the board reported to Howard Lodge on September 7, 1903, they found "the buildings and premises in better repair than they have been in years. The Board instructed the Principal to put water in for the use of the college." [79]

During the next year Griffin complied with the board's instruction and was able to "put water in" for a total expenditure of $72.18.[80] He also made repairs to the buildings at a cost of $99.55 and reported to the board: "The condition of the building is fairly good, though much work should be done in order to make it as good as the average modern school building. Every dollar of the money is needed, and much more could be used in order to make the building as near as possible like modern school buildings." [81]

The board of visitors made its annual report and transmitted President Griffin's report to Howard Lodge, October 31, 1904:

> In as much as there have recently been added to Howard Lodge quite a number of valuable members and we rejoice in this we desire to call the attention of the Lodge to the part that Howard Female College is over a half century old, and stands as the only Odd Fellows School in the world and as the splendid old School stands under the guardian care and protection aegis, the Odd Fellows of the world and especially of Howard Lodge. We must earnestly insist that every member of this Lodge, give his hearty support and co-operation to the upbuilding, and advancement of the best interest of this school, one of the cardinal tenets of our

---

[76] *Howard Minute Book, 1885-1905*, p. 304.
[77] *Ibid.*, p. 323.
[78] *Ibid.*, p. 355.
[79] *Ibid.*, p. 374.
[80] *Ibid.*, p. 403.
[81] *Ibid.*, p. 404.

beloved order is to educate the orphans and during its fifty years cared for more than scores of the orphans of our brethren have enjoyed the munificent bounty of this splendid institution and during the past year, Prof. Griffin report shows that two orphans have attended this school.

Trusting that Howard College may share in the splendid growth that is now attending our beloved order in Tennessee, and every true and Loyal Odd Fellow will rally to her support, we in Friendship Love and Truth submit the foregoing reports.

> JAMES W. BLACKMORE, *President*
> J. T. BASKERVILLE, *Secretary*
> GEO. W. BODDIE
> P. L. ANDERSON
> A. J. SWANEY
> W. F. ALBRIGHT

Prof. Z. K. Griffin's Report President of Howard College.
The building of Howard College is insured as follows.

Insurance Co of North America	$2,800.00
Phoenix	2,000.00
Hartford	2,500.00
Hartford	1,875.00
Total	$9,175.00

The condition of the building is fairly good, though much work should be done in order to make it as good as the average moderne School building. Every Dollar of the money is needed, and much more could be used in order to make the building as near as possible like modern school buildings. The year which closed last June was the most successful of the school since it has been in the hands of the present management.

The number of pupils enrolled in the literary department	110
The number of pupils enrolled special work	15
Total in attendance	125

The opening of the school for the term of 1904 & 1905 is good, and now promises to be better than last year with the influence of the Lodge and support of our home people, I think we can have as many as our building will accommodate. In submitting the above report I wish to ask that every Odd Fellow do what he can for the school.

> Respectfully,
> Z. K. GRIFFIN[82]

---

[82] *Ibid.,* p. 403.

Catalogs published by Howard Female College, not unlike those of other educational institutions in Middle Tennessee, consistently recommended the healthy climate of the area. The catalog of 1907, calling attention to the four acres of campus "which is shaded by large forest trees," stated: "Girls are permitted and urged to spend most of their leisure time outdoors on the campus." Whether this was a testimonial to the mildness of the winter weather or to the hardiness of Howard's "young ladies" was not indicated.[83]

From 1906 to 1908 A. L. Edwards served as President of Howard Female College in the place of Z. K. Griffin. Edwards, who held an A.B. degree from Vanderbilt University, enlarged the library and made the reading room one of the most attractive features of the school. During his tenure, a modern athletic program was developed for the students.[84]

In 1908 H. H. Savage replaced Edwards and soon afterward helped launch a campaign to install a modern heating plant and to repair and redecorate the college building. The heating facility installed by Professor Burney years earlier had failed in 1907 and the building was generally in need of repairs and decorating. Most of the news columns of the Sumner County *News*, April 1, 1909, were devoted to the college and its need for modern equipment and repairs. Professor Savage contributed an article stating the school's needs and proposing an answer to the question: What does Howard College need? He wrote, ". . . the college should be re-papered, painted on the outside, walls repaired, additional baths, laboratory for class room work, more desks, and a steam heating plant. . . . The college cannot compete with other schools either in prices or advantages in its present condition. We must have what competing schools have or close." George W. Boddie, chairman of the board of visitors, wrote of the "Financial Advantages of Howard College to this Community From an Educational Standpoint." He concluded that local families would face much higher costs of education should they send their daughters to out of town institutions and that the demise of Howard Col-

---

[83] Sumner County *News,* March 9, 1961.
[84] *Ibid.,* August 13, 1931.

lege would adversely affect the local economy. "We think . . . that our people should become aroused . . . to the . . . important fact . . . that there is a need of their assistance without which this beneficent institution is sadly crippled, cannot prosper and may go down." That Howard College was facing hard times was further indicated by the size of the graduating class of 1909—only six young ladies.[85] The board of visitors for 1909 were, in addition to Boddie, J. M. Ashburn, James W. Blackmore, W. F. Albright, D. B. Puryear, and Dan Gaines.

The results of the drive to improve the college in 1909 are not specifically known, but the efforts were productive enough to keep the school open. A newspaper notice appeared August 19 announcing that the college would open September 15 and that two concerts had been scheduled there by the Nashville Military Band. Readers were reminded of Howard's strong conservatory of music and the attention devoted to it by President Savage, himself a graduate of Boston Conservatory of Music and the Royal Conservatory, Berlin, Germany. Mrs. Savage and Misses Matthews and Dasher were mentioned as teachers in the department.[86] This special promotion of Howard's music department was undoubtedly the result of a growing hostility between President Savage and Mrs. Prudence Simpson Dresser, a former teacher at Howard who had left to form her own conservatory, the Dresser School of Music. Mrs. Dresser's music school, located three short city blocks away, had grown substantially since its opening and had consistently attracted students who otherwise would have enrolled at Howard College. During the remainder of the school year, Savage and Mrs. Dresser publicly exchanged pointed unpleasantries. On April 21, 1910, Savage, agreeing to complete the school term, resigned as President of Howard College. It was immediately announced that his successor would be Walter Aurelius Ingram, a 31-year-old native of North Carolina who had been teaching at Harlem, Georgia, when he was selected to come to Gallatin.[87] Both Savage and Ingram participated

---

[85] *Ibid.*, April 29, 1909.
[86] *Ibid.*, August 19, 1909.
[87] *Ibid.*, April 21, 1910.

in the commencement program in late May, 1910,[88] and Savage departed soon thereafter. The bitter rivalry that had developed between him and Mrs. Dresser was still a part of the public scene June 9 when a letter from "a Peacemaker" appeared in the Sumner County *News* bearing the suggestion that Savage and Mrs. Dresser should submit their credentials to a committee of three whose judgment of their respective merit they would accept as final.

By the opening of the school year 1910-1911, President Ingram had dressed up the annual catalog by the use of attractive photographs of the campus and smiling students. Scattered between the impressive illustrations were pages of pertinent facts about Howard College. The college had maintained its relationship with the Grand Lodge of Tennessee. Its situation was explained: "The college buildings and grounds belong to Howard Lodge No. 13, I.O.O.F., at Gallatin, Tennessee, and the College is under the auspices of the Grand Lodge of Tennessee. The relation of the Order to the College is, therefore, that of a fostering patron; but it extends the same privileges to all students, regardless of church relation or section. Free tuition is given in the Literary Department to all worthy orphans of the Order." [89] The members of the board of visitors from the Grand Lodge were listed: Mrs. Alice Edelen, president, Knoxville; Miss Theresa A. Cramer, secretary, Nashville; M. M. Summer, Lewisburg; Jesse Henson, Knoxville; and J. R. Harwell, Nashville. The Howard Lodge board members were George W. Boddie, Dr. J. M. Ashburn, James W. Blackmore, D. B. Puryear, W. F. Albright, and Dan Gaines.[90]

The students of Howard College were advised in advance of the dress code on campus: the girls would wear a uniform. "This will consist of a tailor suit of a dark blue cloth, to be worn with a white shirt waist. A black oxford cap will be worn . . . our pupils will wait until they come to school to supply themselves. We will be able to secure the suits at a price not exceeding eigh-

---

[88] *Ibid.*, May 26, 1910.
[89] *Howard Female College Catalog, 1910-1911.*
[90] *Ibid.*

teen dollars, and our boarding pupils will be expected to wear them at all times when they leave the college premises and on public occasions." [91]

Under Ingram's leadership the administration and board of visitors adopted the slogan of "A New and Greater Howard" as the school's rallying cry.[92] Enthusiasm was so high when school opened that a local editor was moved to proclaim: "The faculty for the present year is one of unusual strength in every department and the outlook for 'A New and Greater Howard' is indeed bright." [93]

Howard's auspicious 1910 opening was soon over-shadowed by the events of a year that saw the faculty torn by dissension. Two certain results of the dispute were the resignations of President Ingram and a faculty member, Miss Patti Malone. When Ingram had left town Miss Malone was persuaded to rejoin the faculty.

By early August, 1911, W. H. Buck had become president of Howard College. A graduate of Ohio Normal University, Buck had been president of Lexington Female College, Lexington, Missouri, and had been superintendent of city schools at Ardmore, Oklahoma, and Gulfport, Mississippi.[94]

Near the end of Buck's first year, he seemed to have rekindled local interest in Howard College. A newspaper editorial May 9, 1912, commended plans of the Howard Alumnae Association to raise funds to improve the chapel. But the editor, also, pointed out that the improvement plans should be extended to the entire facility so that Howard's buildings would compare favorably with those of other colleges in the area.[95] Howard Lodge joined in the action by getting pledges of cooperation from Grand Lodge representatives in seeking financial support for the college from other I.O.O.F. lodges in Tennessee.[96]

Although little improvement money had been raised by the opening of the new school term in September, President Buck

[91] Sumner County *News,* March 9, 1961.
[92] *Ibid.,* July 21, 1910.
[93] *Ibid.,* September 15, 1910.
[94] *Ibid.,* August 10, 1911.
[95] *Ibid.,* May 9, 1912.
[96] *Ibid.,* May 16, 1912.

was greeted by the largest boarding school enrollment in recent years. But the presence of boarding students—even in goodly number—was not enough to make ends meet for the administration. Sometime in March, 1913, Buck gave notice of his resignation that would become effective at the end of the school year, two months hence.

President Buck's capitulation again focused local attention on the financially harassed college. The Commercial Club, a new organization of local businessmen and a forerunner of the Gallatin Chamber of Commerce, set out to raise $5,000 for Howard by calling a public rally for the evening of April 3, 1913. That the college was fighting for its life was evident from newspaper promotion of the rally which included the admonition: "We must not allow Howard College to be lost to this community." [97]

In less than two weeks the Commercial Club had raised over $5,000. On April 24, the total in the fund stood at $6,700.[98] At this point, Mrs. Carolina Polk Horton of Nashville, a niece of General Leonidas Polk, one of the founders of the University of the South at Sewanee, Tennessee, became the first woman president of Howard Female College when she agreed to reorganize the school for the beginning of the school year 1913-1914. Mrs. Horton's faculty members for the first year were Misses Susan Josephine Summers, Ruth Morris Welles, Rebecca Edward Jones, Elleanor Margaret Welles, Alice Ramsey, Eleanor Powers Newman, Pauline Magness, Lena D. Fritts, Gladys Dean, Ella Sophronestia Hergesheimer, and Mary Harrison Herbrick. Howard College continued "under the auspices of the Grand Lodge of Tennessee . . . fostering patron" and continued to be closely observed and guided by a board of visitors from Howard Lodge. The visitors for 1914-1915 were George W. Boddie, Dr. J. M. Ashburn, James W. Blackmore, W. G. Schamburger, R. M. Whiteside, and Ernest Franklin.[99]

Mrs. Horton operated the college for three years. Her resignation, prompted by inadequate operating revenues, was announced

[97] *Ibid.,* April 3, 1913.
[98] *Ibid.,* April 24, 1913.
[99] *Howard College Catalog, 1914-1915.*

May 11, 1916. She was followed at the beginning of the school year 1916-1917 by J. H. Hatton of St. Louis who was reputed "to control abundant resources to finance the school." [100] Hatton, regarded by Howard's board of visitors as a stable man for the helm of the college, signed a ten-year lease on the school property and moved to Gallatin. His first year at Howard passed quietly; but before the beginning of the second, he had decided to advertise his school to the public. Before the fall term of school opened on September 13, 1917, President Hatton published the names of his faculty members: Stewart P. Hatton, associate president, Latin and history; Miss Marcia L. Buchholz, Peabody College, English and art; Miss Mildred Fowler, University of Chattanooga, English; Miss Gwendolyn Webster, Kearney (Nebraska) State Normal, domestic science and intermediate department; Miss Carrie Briggs Whiteside, Peabody College, French and primary; Miss Winifred Spence, University of Chattanooga, history and mathematics; Miss Ethyll Weems, Kearney State Normal, critic teacher in primary; Mrs. M. Price, director, voice and piano; Mrs. P. E. Hatton, associate director; and Miss Ann P. Wright, expression. It was also announced that Miss Susie Green had been elected Matron and that the name of "a fine teacher of violin and orchestral instruments" would be released as soon as "arrangements have been consummated." [101]

On the opening day of school, President Hatton predicted an increase in enrollment over the previous year and assured his patrons that the school was here to stay. Striking at the foes of the college, he stated: "There are well laid plans for the maintenance and upbuilding of Howard College through the present and through coming years, notwithstanding designedly evil prophecies and reports to the contrary."

Recognizing that the number of schools competing for public support had increased during the last quarter century, Hatton observed: "There is room in Gallatin for all our schools. Each offers enough of that which the others can not to justify the main-

---

[100] Sumner County *News*, May 11, 1916.
[101] *Ibid.*, August 30, 1917.

tenance of all. One gains nothing in the end by seeking to injure one that another may gain some imaginary advantage." [102]

A large and improved attendance had materialized at Howard College by the end of September and the school was adjudged by editor Edward Albright to have bright prospects ahead.[103] Accounts of various literary, social and athletic events at Howard appeared frequently in the local press during the autumn of 1917. But the momentum that Hatton seemed to be developing soon lost its thrust. During the summer of 1918, President Hatton yielded his lease to the lodge. The Sumner County *News*, August 15, 1918, announced that Dr. George H. Crowell, president of Logan College, Russellville, Kentucky, would become head of Howard College "at once." The newspaper also stated without elaboration, "Prof. and Mrs. Hatton and Mrs. Price will leave immediately for California where they will reside."

During his first year at Howard, Crowell, whose credentials included the Ph.B. degree from the University of North Carolina and the Ph.D. from Central University, seems to have found the plant in a deteriorating condition and the school itself in jeopardy.

He lost no time in planning a "rehabilitation" of the college.[104] First, he determined that Howard Female College would offer instruction in the standard twelve grades plus the freshman and sophomore levels of a "grade A college." [105] Crowell next announced his faculty for 1918-1919, all of whom were newcomers to the local scene: President Crowell, Bible and ethics; Miss Helen Horton, A.B., Hendrix College, Conway Arkansas, mathematics, science and English; Miss Ruby Loyd, A.B., Southern College, Latin, French, history; Miss Rebecca Porter, A.B., University of Nashville, high school; Miss Clara Belle DeHaven, A.B., Froehel and Pestalozzi School, Chicago, kindergarten and primary; Mrs. Della Gilbert, M.B., New England Conservatory, Boston, piano and voice; Mrs. Florence Kierluff Kennon, M.E.,

---

[102] *Ibid.*, September 13, 1917.
[103] *Ibid.*, September 30, 1917.
[104] *Ibid.*, August 29, 1918.
[105] *Ibid.*, September 5, 1918.

Henderson Brown College, Arkadelphia, Arkansas, expression, violin, and art; Miss Irene Long, Logan College, Russellville, Kentucky, stenography, bookkeeping, typewriting.[106]

The first response to Dr. Crowell and his faculty was, at best, lukewarm. Ten days after the opening of school he had enrolled only 59 students, although it was reported that there were "more in prospect." [107] A bold stroke was needed and Crowell thought that an extension or expansion program requiring the provision of substantial capital funds from local sources might supply the drama that he sought. Before the year passed the new president had taken the lead in launching a campaign to raise $30,000 to repair the school facilities and to acquire four adjacent parcels of land. Just over $34,000 was subscribed during the solicitation that was triumphantly closed in the late summer of 1919. Inspired by this unprecedented success in raising funds, speakers at the opening of school in September, 1919, not surprisingly proclaimed it "the Best, the largest and the most enthusiastic within the history of the college." [108]

The public enthusiasm generated during the fund drive seems to have created the kind of interest in the college that Dr. Crowell sought. Enrollment increased dramatically to a total of 130 young women, and he, like others before him, raised the cry for more room. "We are now crowded. We are teaching in the office, in the hall, in the study hall, in a bed room, in the library. How supremely we need . . . the Home Economics in its allotted space, the Science Hall or laboratory fitted up; the study hall relieved of recitation work and made a place of quiet study under a superintendent." [109]

The successful capital funds drive had been achieved by promising subscribers that they would receive shares of stock in Howard College Extension Corporation. Once the subscriptions had been made, the corporation was duly organized and its officers elected. They were C. G. McLean, president; John B. Swaney, treasurer;

[106] *Ibid.*, September 5, 1918.
[107] *Ibid.*, September 26, 1918.
[108] *Bulletin, Howard College, 1919-1920.*
[109] *Ibid.*

and George H. Crowell, secretary. By February 12, 1920, the stock certificates were signed and ready for distribution and subscribers were urged to come forward and make good their subscriptions.[110]

Most of the money pledged to Howard College through its Extension Corporation was earmarked for purchasing adjoining real estate. During 1919 and 1920 four acquisitions were made which added impressively to the college's campus. Immediately east of the college a house and lot belonging to Mrs. Alice T. Foster were purchased for $6,500. The Foster property had a frontage extending 110 feet along East Main Street and was bounded on the rear or south side by Smith Street.[111] East of this parcel was the Methodist parsonage property extending 90 feet along East Main Street and also bounded on the rear by Smith Street. It was acquired from the Gallatin Methodist Episcopal Church South for $5,500.[112] The old "Main Street public school property" which adjoined the Methodist parsonage lot was bought from the Sumner Hotel Company for $12,961.74. This lot extended 110½ feet along East Main Street, was bounded on the east by "the Ewing property" and on the south or rear by Smith Street. Located on this site was a school building that is yet standing and, now remodeled, is known as the Hillcrest Apartments.[113] A fourth purchase added a lot and brick building formerly used by the Gallatin Christian Church as a house of worship. It was located at the southwest corner of the campus, was bounded on the west by Boyers Street, on the south by Smith Street, and on the north by the First Baptist Church lot.[114]

The real estate purchases more than doubled the size of the college campus. It is no wonder that President Crowell, writing in his capacity as secretary of the Extension Corporation, was excited about the impact of this expansion of the college plant. "This would give Gallatin a plant that would catch the eye of all Tennessee and adjoining states and strike the hearts of every-

[110] Sumner County *News*, February 12, 1920.
[111] *SCR, Deed Book #82*, p. 610.
[112] *SCR, Deed Book #84*, p. 310.
[113] *SCR, Deed Book #82*, p. 610.
[114] *SCR, Deed Book #95*, p. 446.

body with our ability to see and to realize a good thing and our zeal and determination to accomplish it." [115]

During the second year of Crowell's administration, the college continued to offer work in its "Collegiate Department" where a "Junior College" diploma could be obtained. Howard's four years of high school education prepared students "for entrance either into the Collegiate Department of Howard College or for entrance into any other college in the country." [116] All female graduates from high schools in Gallatin and Sumner County were declared acceptable for Howard's Junior College course. Education in the lower or elementary grades was also offered.

The faculty of Howard College for the school year 1919-1920 included, in addition to Crowell,[117] his wife, Mrs. George H. Crowell, superintendent of the boarding school; Miss Elizabeth Billingslea, Miss Clara Belle DeHaven, Miss Evelina McCauley, Miss Susia May Keathley, Mrs. Florence Kierluff Kennon, Miss Afra Kirsch, Miss Lucile Shinnick, Miss Cathryn Irene Long, Miss Virginia Beck, and Miss Caroline Snyder.

During the winter term, 1919-1920, there were 145 young ladies enrolled at the college, 40 of whom were boarding students. The Sumner County *News* was jubilant: "This success, when it is considered how dead the College was a year and a half ago . . . is enough to . . . fill the hearts of all the friends of the college." [118] The upward trend in enrollment continued so that by commencement time in June there were 150 students at Howard.[119]

Renovation of the gymnasium and construction of a large swimming pool were among the several improvements initiated during the summer.[120] Work on these and other projects contemplated in the Extension Corporation program was completed

---

[115] Sumner County *News*, February 12, 1920.

[116] *Bulletin, Howard College, 1919-1920.*

[117] The president taught Latin and explained its importance to Howard's curriculum: "I am teaching all of the Latin myself and am seeking to make it, verily, a *live language. It is alive. It is living and speaking out in pure diction,* and *liquid phrases, from myriads of tongues.* . . . The *girls* are fond of *Latin." Ibid.*

[118] Sumner County *News*, February 19, 1920.

[119] *Ibid.,* June 10, 1920.

[120] *Ibid.,* July 29, 1920.

in early 1921.[121]

As surely as August brought the traditional "dog days" of summer, it also brought the annual announcement of the faculty of Howard Female College. For the year 1920-1921, Dr. Crowell would teach Bible, logics, ethics, psychology, and pedagogy; Elizabeth Billingslea, history and English; Evelina McCauley, science and modern languages; Zada Holliman, commercial course and mathematics; Susia May Keathley, Latin and grammar grades; Mary E. Copenhaver, art and intermediate and grammar grades; Willard Freeman, home economics and intermediate and grammar grades; Mazie McLane, kindergarten and elementary school; Afra Brandon Kirsch, voice and piano; Leland D. Smith, piano; Nell Bate, piano; Mary Margaret Chester, fine arts; Lorraine Sullivan would be librarian and Mrs. Myrtle Dobson, nurse.[122]

In spite of the great achievements of Howard Female College in plant extension and improvement, the opening of the fall term brought out only about 100 students, some 50 less than had completed the previous year's work.[123] Yet Dr. Crowell and his faculty seem to have worked perseveringly during the entire school year. Their students were exposed to the public in plays, YMCA activities, concerts, festivals, recitals, examinations, and traditional commencement observances. Even the college athletic program attracted statewide attention when its basketball team completed a ten game schedule without defeat and entered claim to the state championship! [124] But there was no way to conceal the fact that at the end of the school year, there were only four graduates from the junior college program and thirteen graduates of the high school department.[125]

Faced with the old problem of revenue deficiencies, President Crowell determined to assemble a student body of sufficient size to fund the operating budget for 1921-1922. With the local area seemingly unable to supply students enough to sustain the school,

[121] *Ibid.*, May 12, 1921.
[122] *Ibid.*, August 12, 1920.
[123] *Ibid.*, September 16, 1920.
[124] *Ibid.*, March 31, 1921.
[125] *Ibid.*, June 9, 1921.

the president packed his bags and, during the summer months, traveled extensively in Middle Tennessee and Southern Kentucky telling the story of Howard Female College. Readers of the Sumner County *News* found Crowell so busy extolling the virtues of his school and reporting the prospects of new students from nearby counties that he failed to prepare his annual faculty announcement.

In September, Howard opened its doors for what turned out to be its last full year of operation. Notwithstanding Dr. Crowell's summer travels, there seems to have been little increase in the size of the student body. The number of graduates declined to a total of three from the college and eight from the high school department. It seemed so hopeless that on June 29 Crowell tendered his resignation to the board of visitors.[126]

The board of visitors was not ready to admit defeat and, after a meeting with Crowell, announced that his resignation had been rejected. The president agreed to remain at his post and soon afterward began preparations for the school to be opened in September.[127]

But the tide was running against Crowell and private schools generally. The full impact of public schools and state colleges, while yet to be felt, was foreshadowed by the decline of scores of private schools funded largely or entirely by tuition payments. When only fifty girls enrolled for the fall term at Howard, Crowell knew that he could not continue. On October 6, 1922, George H. Crowell resigned the presidency of Howard College, dissolved its faculty and closed its doors. The tuition paid by fifty students was not sufficient to pay expenses.[128]

The board of visitors of the college accepted Crowell's resignation and hopefully promised to try to engage someone in his place by the beginning of the next school year. But when Crowell resigned, the doors of Howard Female College were closed never to be opened again over the threshold of a private institution.

What happened to Howard Female College? Dr. Crowell pro-

---

[126] *Ibid.*, June 29, 1922.
[127] *Ibid.*, July 6, 1922.
[128] *Ibid.*, October 12, 1922.

vided his answer in a farewell letter to the Sumner County *News* in which he admitted that:

> We have fought a losing game as did the men of proud Dixie, and are forced now in humility and embarrassment to give up the work in defeat on account of: first, a lack of the proper cooperation on the part of those able to cooperate; second, the lack of the proper community pride, spirit and interest that the living, throbbing, building, growing communities possess; thirdly, because of the influence of millions expended in the educational activities of the various denominations; and fourthly, because of hard conditions brought about by the World War, the high cost of living and uncertainty and the high price of coal; fifthly, because of the continuous and insistent opposition and competition on the part of free public schools and normals—thus making our matriculations this fall insufficient to pay the salaries and expenses for the year.[129]

Dr. Crowell's reasons for the demise of Howard Female College seem logical enough, although he seems to have listed them in inverse order of importance. The college depended on a substantial enrollment of pre-college students. It was by the loss of many of this group to the improving public schools that irreparable financial damage was done to Howard. The citizens of Gallatin and surrounding areas had periodically rallied to the support of Howard College for seventy-five years. But this time the rally failed to materialize.

After the college was closed, the campus and the main building were used by the public schools until 1931 when the building, a part of which had been erected in 1837, was demolished. In its place a new public school structure was erected to house Howard Elementary School. Thus the name of Howard College has been perpetuated in the public school system of Sumner County and classes continue to be held on the site on East Main Street where young ladies have attended schools—of one kind or another—for over 150 years. Among the cornerstone memorabilia of Howard Elementary School, there was included a history of Howard Female College written by Mrs. Kate Todd Malone, whose father, Hugh Blair Todd, was a former president of the college.

[129] *Ibid.*

1. The large classroom and dormitory complex occupied by Howard Female College was located on the present site of Howard Elementary School, East Main Street, Gallatin. Occupants of the facility included the Gallatin Female Academy (1837-1838), Sumner Female Academy (1838-1856), Howard Female Institute (1856-1861), and Howard Female College thereafter except for the period 1874-1878 when its occupant was Neophogen Male and Female College.

2. The campus of Howard Female College is shown as it was photographed for the yearbook of 1905. The First Baptist Church building is at the right rear of the picture and just left of center is the bell tower of a building first used as a factory, later as a church and finally as a gymnasium for Howard Female College. Most of the young ladies appear to be dressed in the school uniform consisting of a white blouse and long blue skirt.

3. Now the Hillcrest Apartments, this two-story brick building served early in this century as the faculty dormitory for Howard Female College. Its location adjoined the main campus on East Main Street in Gallatin. It is the only building still standing that was once a part of Howard Female College.

4. Joseph Smith Fowler, president of Howard Female Institute 1857-1861, was a staunch Unionist. He was treasurer of the State of Tennessee during the latter years of the Civil War and was elected to the United States Senate immediately prior to Tennessee's readmission to the Union after the war. He was a member of the Senate during President Andrew Johnson's impeachment trial and voted to acquit the President.

5. Isaac Franklin, whose portrait above was done in oils for the family, provided through his will for a large bequest to endow Isaac Franklin Institute. The school was to have been located on his beautiful Fairvue property in Sumner County. Litigation initiated by his widow finally succeeded in breaking his will and aborting the school.

HOWARD FEMALE COLLEGE

·Gallatin· Tennessee.

ELEVATION OF OLD FRONT, REMODELED.
HOWARD FEMALE COLLEGE, GALLATIN, TENN.

NEW FRONT—ELEVATION

This Certifies, that Miss _____

having completed the full course of

ENGLISH LITERATURE AND MATHEMATICS

prescribed by this Institution, and having passed satisfactory Examinations in the same,

is entitled to this

DIPLOMA

Awarded by the Faculty and Board of Visitors of Howard Female College,

with the honors of the Degree of Mistress of English Literature.

In Testimony of which we have affixed our signatures and the Seal of the College.

Given at the College, this the 2ᵈ day of June, 1887. June 30 College Campus.

L. M. Burney   President of Faculty

B. F. Allen   President of Board of Visitors

E. A. Buchanan   Secretary Board of Visitors

6. This Howard Female College diploma was issued to the late Vena H. Stuart of Gallatin June 2, 1887. It conferred upon her the degree of Mistress of English Literature. The diploma was signed by A. M. Burney, President of the Faculty, and B. F. Allen, President of the Board of Visitors. Vena Stuart Elementary School, Gallatin, is named in her honor.

7. *The present residence of Mr. and Mrs. John Garrott, East Main Street, Gallatin, was used as the boys' dormitory of Neophogen Male and Female College from 1874 to 1878. The house was built sometime between 1829 and 1841 by Levy D. King, one-time president of Transmontania Academy, a local boys' school.*

8. *John M. Walton, president of Neophogen Male and Female College, is shown as he appeared in the school's catalog for 1874-75. His failure to add a necktie to his otherwise formal attire prompted a satirical review of the catalog by the* Nation *magazine.*

9. Tullatuskee Normal College at Bethpage, Tennessee, was organized for teacher training; but, as in the case of Harry M. Senter, successful completion of the Commercial Course led to the Degree of Bachelor of Accounts. His diploma was signed by E. B. Wilson and Pattie Malone for the faculty and by J. B. Hanner for the Board of Trustees.

10. *The impressive proportions of the first building planned for the campus of the Pythian College are shown in a rendering by its architect Jules G. Zwicker of Nashville. This structure was to have been located near the center of a 30-acre campus on North Water Street, Gallatin, one mile north of the public square.*

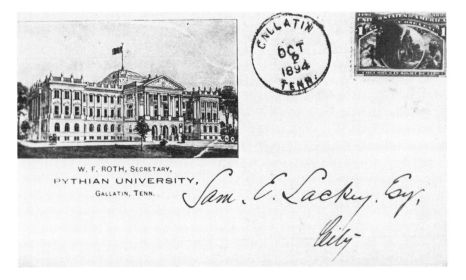

11. *The Pythian College movement was started in Gallatin by the local Rowena Lodge, Knights of Pythias. The envelope shown here was specially imprinted for use by Rowena Lodge in promoting the college. It is addressed to S. E. Lackey, a local member of the order.*

12. *A remnant of the Pythian College cornerstone shows that it was dedicated May 2, 1894. The dedication ceremonies were attended by a large corps of Knights of Pythias. Members and officers arrived by special train from Nashville where the annual state convention was then in progress.*

13. *Students and visitors are welcomed to its campus by this sign at the entrance to Volunteer State Community College, Gallatin.*

14. *Dr. Hal Reed Ramer became the first President of Volunteer State Community College in July, 1970. He was formerly Assistant Commissioner for Higher Education in Tennessee and, earlier, was Assistant to the President of Ohio State University.*

15. The 100-acre campus of Volunteer State Community College is shown in this aerial photograph. Located on U.S. Highway 31-E at Gallatin, it overlooks to the south the ante-bellum Fairvue plantation of Isaac Franklin. A new classroom building is under construction on the west side of the campus. Its facilities, including a small theatre, will soon be added to those of the four original buildings erected in 1970-71.

CHAPTER III

NEOPHOGEN MALE AND FEMALE COLLEGE

ONE OF THE first college-level institutions in the South to practice coeducation was Neophogen Male and Female College, founded at nearby Cross Plains in Robertson County in 1873 and removed to Gallatin in 1874 by John M. Walton, its founder.[1] The relocation to Gallatin came in the aftermath of a destructive fire that razed the new main building at Cross Plains.

In the 1870's there were still very few institutions in the United States that granted college degrees to coeds. Mt. Union College, Alliance, Ohio, the first school in the country to award the A.B. and B.S. degrees to full time coeds, had granted a total of only 28 degrees to its women students by 1874 while it had awarded 167 degrees to young men during the same period.[2]

Walton set up his Neophogen College in the facilities that had previously housed Howard Female College. Although he assiduously avoided any reference to the name Howard, he leased the land and buildings from Howard Lodge in much the same way that earlier educators had done. The coeds lived in the dormitory quarter of the old Howard College main building while the male students were lodged a city block away in a large two story residence at 332 East Main Street.[3] Walton had, apparently, rented

---

[1] John M. Walton, son of Thomas J. and Martha Bartlett Walton, was born in Robertson County, Tennessee, May 7, 1839. His father was a medical doctor at Cross Plains. At age 14 John entered Franklin College at Franklin, Tennessee, where he remained for two years. He spent the next three years at school in Virginia and then returned to the Law School of Cumberland University, Lebanon, Tennessee. He was graduated from Cumberland in 1859. In 1861 Walton enlisted in the Seventh Tennessee Cavalry and participated in the Battle of Shiloh. Soon afterward he was forced out of military service by bad health. In 1866 he began a teaching career at Cross Plains that led in 1873 to the establishment there of his dream school—Neophogen Male and Female College. When fire wrecked the college during its first year, he removed it to Gallatin. *History of Tennessee, From the Earliest Time to the Present* (Nashville: The Goodspeed Publishing Co., 1887), p. 1197.

[2] Newell Yost Osborne, *A Select School, Mt. Union College* (Alliance, Ohio, 1967), p. 65.

[3] Now the home of Mr. and Mrs. John Garrott of Gallatin.

or leased the house from its owners for use as a dormitory. In 1873 and for sometime thereafter, it was owned by four men who became members of Neophogen's honorary board of visitors in 1874: George W. Allen, James J. Turner, Thomas Boyers, and Samuel Nickelson.

D. C. Beers' detailed map of Sumner County,[4] published in 1878, incorrectly listed the residence and property at 332 East Main Street as "Howard Male College." The map-maker's confusion was consistent as he labeled the Neophogen campus "Howard Female College." His confusion was, in fact, shared and perpetuated by the townspeople who were accustomed to the name Howard and who, in many cases, found the name Neophogen too formidable even to pronounce.

But Walton was unyielding in his decision to use the name that he had selected for the opening of his college at Cross Plains a year earlier: Neophogen, which translated was "new-light-producing" and which proclaimed to all his determination to have a new-light-producing college.

Part of the new light to be produced by Walton's school seems to have been coeducation. From the first of the four years that he managed to keep the college alive in Gallatin, Walton advertised and practiced coeducation. Although carefully segregated by sexes, young men and women were on the same campus, sometimes attended the same classes, and were granted like degrees for like work.

That Tennessee during reconstruction years needed new-light-producing education can hardly be doubted. There were, however, few indications of what else might have been expected from Neophogen to distinguish it from other colleges of its period. The school had a "National Idea" and Walton wrote briefly of it in the catalog of 1875: "No Text-book of a sectional bias is taught in Neophogen, and no sectional ideas inculcated by the teachers; who with the students here from the two great sections

---

[4] *Map of Sumner County, Tennessee,* D. C. Beers and Company, Philadelphia, Pennsylvania, 1878.

of our common country, move along harmoniously together." [5]
The school, as revealed in its catalogs and advertisements, seems
otherwise to have been typically southern and conservative with
emphasis on etiquette, strict codes of social behavior, and classical
studies.

With the files of Gallatin newspapers of the Neophogen period
burned and only scattered copies in existence, a week-to-week
story of the college seems unlikely to be pieced together. Yet a
few scrapbook clippings and the school catalogs, published in 1875
and 1877, provide helpful insights into life at Neophogen.

A surviving copy of the Gallatin *Examiner,* May 7, 1875, relates
a story of "Neophogen and May."

> The students of Neophogen College had a delightful May
> festival last Friday night at the college Building . . . a large crowd
> was present and was greatly delighted with the scene.

After listing the "programme" with both its male and female
performers, the newspaper continued its account:

> The ceremony was performed in beautiful style. The Queen,
> Miss Cooke, was most royally attired, and well became her regal
> position, bearing herself with great self-possession and dignity. The
> attendants were, also, charmingly costumed, and everything was
> done in good taste.
> After the crowning of the Queen, the large hall was cleared for
> dancing; and the young folks enjoyed themselves to a late hour,
> under the inspiring music of Ewing's band from Nashville.

Six weeks later, the first year of Neophogen College drew to a
close. The *Examiner* reported the concluding events in its edition
of June 18, 1875:

> On Monday afternoon the public literary exercises, embracing
> orations by the young men, reading of essays, etc. commenced and
> was continued until a late hour in the evening. The charades were
> performed pleasantly and with spirit, while the Tableaux Vivant
> were charmingly presented by the young ladies and gentlemen of
> the College.

---

[5] *Neophogen Male and Female College, Gallatin, Tenn., Semi-Annual Catalogue,*
December, 1875.

On Tuesday evening the hall was crowded to overflowing to hear the performances of the Musical classes of Prof. Sporer and Mrs. Walton . . . it was one of the pleasantest evenings that we have spent for a long time. The performance of the young ladies elicited deserved applause, for they showed the careful and laborious training of their teachers, as well as the industry and talent of the pupils. At a late hour the concert closed and, to gratify the young people, Prof. Walton kindly consented to let them close with a dance. . . . And thus closed the first year of Neophogen College. We are gratified to hear that the prospects for a largely increased attendance next session are promising.

The news report of the closing events at Neophogen made no mention of distasteful conduct by the audience; but a letter, signed "Tourist" and addressed to the local editor, took those present severely to task for "rudeness." The unidentified writer was given forum in the same issue of the *Examiner* under the heading "What Others Say About Us."

In swinging round the circle I switched off at your town Monday night, and as everybody seemed to be going to the closing exercises at the Neophogen College I went too; and in spite of the threatening weather found the hall densely packed: I was told the school under the management of Prof. Walton and his able corps of teachers was in a flourishing condition. The young ladies and gentlemen acquitted themselves very well indeed. Now, I know Gallatin is noted for its pretty and intelligent ladies as well as its polite gentlemen; but the manner in which some of your people conducted themselves that night, was not very well calculated to impress visitors with the super elegance of your society. To be frank with you, I just haven't got language sufficient to express my supreme disgust for the rudeness of some I saw there that night. I have been to Broadway variety shows in New York; Creole masquerade balls in New Orleans; was camped out six months with a Nevada mining company; was captured once by a party of wild Commanche Indians and have seen them in all their drunken hilarity and thought I was prepared for most anything; but I am free to confess that I was not prepared to see an elite crowd submit to a young lady being hissed through her entire speech, and as if to add insult, to injury when the same young lady had the misfortune to get the trail of her dress rolled up in the curtain after reading a prologue, the crowd became perfectly boisterous! Nor was it confined to the rough dement alone, for there were

some who from appearance might have been mistaken for gentlemen and ladies, indulging in very immodest laughter. Sir, I felt
just like I wanted to take the bull by the horns and organize a
police force and if necessary call out the militia and plant a few
cannons. Oh! I was furious, and if I had have stayed there ten
minutes longer I should have exploded. For fear that I might
grow eloquent I will stop.

Yours, as ever, Tourist

Both in newspaper and catalog advertisements, Walton claimed
a longevity for his school that seems at variance with the facts.
He counted the age of Neophogen from 1866 although he
founded it in 1873. He was either embracing the postwar years
of his predecessors at Howard College or counting the entire
span of his own teaching career.

In an advertisement appearing in the Gallatin *Examiner* September 3, 1875, Walton announced that four additional teachers
had joined his faculty for the school year 1875-1876. They were
C. T. Browne, professor of mathematics with 25 years experience
and "the highest testimonials" from the most distinguished educators in Virginia, Kentucky, and Tennessee; Miss A. F. Plaskett,
"of Ohio," teacher of art whose testimonials state "that they
believe her to be the best art teacher in the west"; S. Athanasiades
of the University of Athens, Greece, "who will fill the chair of
ancient and modern languages . . . an able and experienced
teacher"; and J. W. Huey, professor of natural sciences and
astronomy, who "has been especially trained by the President
for years will preside over the Male study hall and exemplify the
principles of Neophogen training and discipline."

The school notice was concluded with an affirmation of Walton's commitment to discipline in his school. It was, he said, "a
cardinal feature" and those interested should "come and see."
Relating discipline to the new-light-producing education, he
challenged: "Anyone wanting light in the highest order of discipline would do well to visit the study halls and recitation
rooms."

With the arrival of autumn, local townspeople began to antici-
pate the opening of school and doubtless eagerly read the follow-

ing observations reported in the Gallatin *Examiner,* September 3: "Students are already beginning to arrive by every train from all parts of the South, and prospects are that the number of students from a distance will far exceed that of any previous year . . . the faculty of the institution is full and complete, and comprises, in the several departments, instructors of culture and experience."

The seemingly bright prospects for Neophogen College as it opened its school year 1875-1876 were suddenly clouded by the worsening of a nation-wide economic depression that created such a scarcity of money that public schools were not opened that fall. On October 29, John Walton offered to allow a credit of one year for tuition "in consideration of the hard times and to meet the immediate wants of the people to their educational interests." [6] Walton's offer was endorsed by the *Examiner*'s editor who described it as "very liberal" and declared that "we doubt not that there will be a large increase in attendance at once." [7]

The principal technique employed by Walton to promote the college and attract students was the wide distribution of catalogs, each typically containing 32 pages and chock full of Neophogen lore. In the autumn of 1876, Walton advertised that he had "20,000 Catalogues for Gratuitous Distribution." [8] The catalogs contained pictures of the honor students from the preceding year along with a picture of President Walton in evening dress but, strangely, without a necktie. In addition, there were rolls listing the students, the names of faculty members and members of the boards of visitors; repeated citations of the advantages that Neophogen offered its students; the all-encompassing aims of the college and its rules and regulations; descriptions of the community and surrounding countryside, and a wide selection of newspaper endorsements of the school.

The semi-annual catalog published in December, 1875, contained interesting vital statistics about the school. The names of 42 men who were members of the honorary board of visitors

---

[6] Gallatin *Examiner,* October 29, 1875.
[7] *Ibid.*
[8] *Ibid.,* October 6, 1876.

were listed and the six members of the active board of visitors were reported to be Wm. Moore, Jno. T. Baber, W. C. Blue, James House, Jo. Miller, and T. H. King, all of Gallatin. There were 107 male and 68 female students—a total of 175 from the states of Tennessee, Kentucky, Minnesota, Arkansas, Texas, Louisiana, Mississippi, Alabama, and Georgia.[9]

The faculty, headed by John M. Walton, President and Professor Belles Lettres, included Mrs. J. M. Walton, Lady Mentor and Mistress of Aesthetics; J. Walton Huey, A.M., Professor Latin and Astronomy; C. T. Browne, A.M., Professor Mathematics; I. J. Morris, A.M. Professor Grammar; Robert Kidd, A.M., Professor Elocution; A. L. Blackman, B.S., Professor Penmanship, Phonography and Bookkeeping; W. D. Corkran, B.S., Professor English Literature and Moral Science; S. Athanasiades, A.M., Professor Greek, German and French; Mrs. A. A. Walton, M.M., Instructress, Piano, Guitar, and Vocal Culture; Miss Josephine Sporer, M.M., Instrumental Music; Miss Julia T. Walton, Instructress of Harp; Miss A. F. Plaskett, M.A., Professor Mistress-Art Department; J. W. Gray, M.D., Professor Hygiene and Medical Jurisprudence; Miss S. C. Coffee, Preceptress; Mrs. M. B. Foote, Mistress of Cuisine and Hygiene; and Huey doubled as Bursar and Corkran as Secretary of Faculty. Law faculty members were S. F. Wilson, B. F. Allen, W. S. Munday, and James W. Blackmore, all prominent Gallatin attorneys.[10]

The community was described in flattering terms and its citizens especially commended: "We claim for the citizens of Gallatin and vicinity that true virtue and magnanimity found alone in the most refined society . . . while we studiously ignore the idea of aristocracy and nobility, our minds are pleasantly associated with dignity and purity." [11]

Attacking the environment surrounding urban colleges, Walton devoted three paragraphs to the advantages of country colleges. He wrote:

---

[9] *Neophogen Male and Female College, Gallatin, Tenn., Semi-Annual Catalogue, December, 1875.*

[10] *Ibid.*

[11] *Ibid.*

Visit institutions of learning in cities; see the indications of impaired health—breathing impure atmosphere; cut off from wholesome exercise; the many evil surroundings, the liability to form all kinds of evil associations; the lassitude; the lustreless eyes. Do they tell you nothing? Here we have health, *nature,* real life, life earnest, and every wholesome stimulus.

Citizens of cities, if you would save your children, *break up their evil associations;* Place them in a pure moral atmosphere. . . . It matters not the order of schools you may have, even if at your door and tuition free; *it will cost you less to send them here than to retain them in your city homes.*

. . . How very few of our city businessmen can, or do devote the time and thought necessary to train their children aright. It is a great work—the responsibility is great; more than all, the labor is great. You can not govern and train your child as well as those who devote all their energies and talents to that one thing.[12]

Through the catalogs compulsory training in Etiquette was promised as was unremitting attention to English grammar and spelling. The variety of academic degrees offered was profuse and included degrees in law and jurisprudence. In 1875 the Rev. John S. Arbuthnot, pastor of the First Presbyterian Church, Gallatin, received the only honorary degree known to have been awarded by Neophogen: Doctor of Divinity.

That the college had "college cottages" as well as unimproved lots for sale was explained: "A few families can be accommodated with houses who wish to board their own children. Terms liberal. . . . Families wishing to purchase lots and improve them are offered liberal inducements." No mention was made of the location of either the cottages or the lots.[13]

A monthly school magazine, *The College Pen,* while "conducted by the students for their mutual improvement in composition," was edited by W. D. Corkran of the faculty. The contents of the magazine seem to have been varied but restrained. "It contains original and instruction dissertations on all scientific subjects; interesting historical narrations—both ancient and modern; imaginative romances, the most chaste; and other entertaining

[12] *Ibid.*
[13] *Neophogen Annual Catalog, 1877-78,* p. 17.

and readable matter, varied to suit the taste of all classes. . . . It is a literary gem in itself." [14]

Probably the most outstanding service rendered by the *Pen* was providing a job as typesetter for a young Kentucky newspaper editor whose work paid his way through school at Neophogen. The ambitious young man was Opie Read, later to become one of the most prolific writers on the American scene. Read was author of 54 books and countless galleys of newspaper copy.

Read, born in Nashville in 1852, had moved with his parents to Gallatin while still a child. His early education was received from "Professor" Bob Durham of Fountain Head who conducted classes in an old log church house in Gallatin. By the time he was twenty-one years old, Read had become editor of *The Patriot*, a weekly newspaper published at Franklin, Kentucky. He left *The Patriot* to enter John Walton's Neophogen in 1874 or 1875. While at Neophogen, Read wrote several newspaper sketches and sold a story to the New York *Mirror*. Surely he contributed to the *Pen*, but it seems that no copies of the "literary gem" have been preserved.

If the strong promotional material set forth on the first thirty pages of a Neophogen College catalog did not convert the reader, he was sure to knuckle under when confronted by pages 31 and 32 on which appeared in fine print a wide selection of newspaper commendations headed "Opinions of the Press." Brief selections of favorable comment from 63 newspapers indicated that the college catalogs had been distributed to widely scattered points.

From Massachusetts the Boston *Courier* was quoted: "President Walton, of Neophogen, deserves the warm support, not only of the people of his section, but of the entire Union." In Wisconsin the *Wood County Reporter* said: "Neophogen stands high in the estimation of scholarly men all over the country. The Faculty numbers many names known to the educational scientific world." At New Orleans the *Times* said of Neophogen: "It offers to youth of both sexes a thorough and complete education in every depart-

[14] *Ibid.*

ment of science and literature. It is, in the full sense of the word, anti-sectarian." [15]

The endorsements continued on and on. The Nashville *Republican Banner* exuded: "The teachers of Neophogen College have the highest national reputation, both as teachers and authors. It is the cheapest college of the kind in the world, and it is the best one for the males and females of the North and South. It is located in a beautiful section of the state, which was selected with great care." Pennsylvania readers of that state's Williamsport *Gazette and Bulletin* found this editoral comment: "The energy and talent which President Walton has heretofore displayed indicate that he will meet his every promise. The corps of professors of Neophogen is said to be thoroughly competent, composed of the best men at home or abroad." [16]

The favorable press reception to Walton's school through its widely circulated catalogs was somewhat offset by a critical review of the semi-annual catalog of December 1875 which was published in the New York weekly magazine, the *Nation*, December 7, 1876. The *Nation's* editor, unable to ignore Walton's extravagant claims, commented derisively:

> It is not our practice to call attention editorially to schools or colleges, but the attractions of the "Neophogen" (or New-Light Producing) "Male and Female College" of Gallatin, Tennessee, seem to us so remarkable that we feel that our rule will, on this occasion, be truly more honored in the breach than in the observance. We hope we have properly translated the President's Greek. The semi-annual catalogue of December, 1875, which now lies before us . . . only came into our hands very recently. . . . [Opening it] We come on lithographed portraits of the eight "honor-students" of the college—four male and four female— headed by that of the President himself, who is apparently a man of commanding presence and ripe culture, though, if we might criticise at all, we should say that his appearance in full evening dress without a cravat is a regrettable departure from what we consider sound and well-established usage. It is the more deplored because "Etiquette" forms a prominent feature in the college

---

[15] *Ibid.*
[16] *Ibid.*

course. Indeed, the catalogue says that "Etiquette is a Specialty, not a matter of choice [in the curriculum] but compulsion," and that "The course of training in it is, in great part, original. Here it is the theory with continued practice. We think we have the politest students in America. The salutation, the bow, the courtesy, the word, the tone, the look, the inflection, vocal and physical, the attitude, the hand, the feet, the spine, and eye are all observed and studied and the students daily exercised in them."

How the Head of a College who observes and studies even the spines of his students, and exercises the students in their spines in the interest of Etiquette, could be guilty of so great a solecism as sitting for his portrait without a necktie, we own puzzles us, but we dare say it can, and when attention is called to it, will be explained. Another "Specialty" is the English language, the neglect of which in our institutions of learning the President justly mourns, and says he "has known many talented and ingenious men possessed of great knowledge, whose contributions to our literary wealth would have been invaluable, yet they were deterred from writing for the public eye in consequence of their imperfect knowledge of English grammar"; and he adds, doubtless having some neighboring seminaries in his eye: "Many graduates from some of the female colleges ought to be introduced to a *very unpopular* [the italics are doubtless sarcasm] little work called the "Elementary Spelling Book," and would," he observes scornfully, "were they to enter this school." In fact, he offered a one-hundred-dollar gold medal in 1873 to any student of a Kentucky or Tennessee college who should beat his students in the English language. We need hardly say that nobody was bold enough to compete for the prize. As regards terms, the college is the "cheapest in America," partly owing to the low prices of necessaries in Sumner County, but mainly to the fact that the President has "broken the shackles of mental servitude and is guided by no landmarks in teaching that reason, common sense, and experience do not approbate," and he justly observes "that price is not an evidence of quality. Plato taught in a grove: Socrates everywhere, and brick and mortar are poor substitutes for talent."

The college, as we have before said, is a coeducator, and enrolled last year about 110 male and about 75 female students, the intercourse between whom, however, seems to us to be unduly restricted, considering the lofty character of the instruction. The sexes study in separate halls, but "the young ladies and gentlemen are permitted, we may say required, to have interviews in the drawing rooms twice in each month," and "the refining, elevating, and stimulating effects of these associations, we are told, "must be seen to be appreciated." Here, as on the subject of the cravat, we must respectfully but firmly dissent from President Walton. We question much whether any young gentleman—we can only answer for our own sex—was ever "stimulated" or "elevated" by a compulsory fortnightly interview with a girl or girls. We of course speak without practical experience of the system, but we put it to the President whether he has not made his statement a little too sweeping, and whether the interviews have taken place with sufficient frequency to enable him to speak with positiveness as to their effects, and whether he has ever tried the voluntary system in his capacious and tasteful parlors. Among the degrees are "M. E. L." (Master or Mistress of the English Language), "B. A. LL." or "M. A. LL." (Bachelor or Maid of the Ancient Languages), "B. P." or "M. P." (Bachelor or Maid of Philosophy), and "B. F. A." or "M. F. A." (Bachelor or Maid of Fine Arts), which requires Music, Drawing, Painting, and Wax work. There are several degrees for Bachelors and Maids besides these, but we have selected the most remarkable and attractive. Honorary degrees, we are glad to perceive, "are only conferred on the *pre-eminently* worthy. . . ."

On the general advantages of the College . . . we hardly feel competent to expatiate, and only wish we could place a copy of the catalogue in the hands of every one of our readers. The Institution is "centrally located between the North and South, the East and the West" (a circumstance which alone would distinguish it from every other college in the world), and is surrounded by scenery to the description of which President Walton's pen, although he is professor of "Belles-Lettres," is evidently not equal, but he does remark that his district "is the land of the poet's dream and the home of the artist's heart"—a very unusual combination, to speak moderately. As to the city of Gallatin, he says that "Health and Wealth are here combined with 3,500 citizens who cannot be surpassed for intelligence and refinement," and he adds, "that no parallel can be found, estimating the population, to the ten first-class turnpikes" that lead into the city. The "combination of health and wealth with 3,500 refined and intelligent citizens" and "ten first-class turnpikes" would suffice to make Gallatin a remarkable place, but this is not all. The President "claims for Gallatin and *its vicinity*" (the italics are ours) "that true virtue and magnanimity found alone in the most refined society. Here," says he, "identity is lost in public spirit"—which must cause some confusion in the streets and on the turnpikes—"here a studious observance of the rights of others is ever manifested."

We confess on reading this we were led to fear that the inhabitants gave themselves airs and tried to live in haughty seclusion from the hardy agriculturists of the surrounding region. But President Walton, doubtless anticipating this morbid anxiety, goes on to explain: "While we studiously ignore the idea of aristocracy and nobility, our minds are pleasantly associated with dignity and purity."

We regret to perceive in the catalogue some evidence that the President's pure and dignified mind is more or less troubled by the low and sordid cares of real-estate speculation, for he offers "liberal terms to families wishing to purchase lots and improve them"; but the momentary pain which this discovery caused us was dissipated completely when we turned the page and our eye rested on the following noble offer to "Learned Men," which we reproduce in full, and with emotion which we make no attempt to conceal:

"Learned men who have failed in business are tendered every inducement to take a life-home here. We intend to take the most active measures to raise a large life-fund for the relief of unfortunate literary men. Let them have homes and the Society of Congenial Spirits."

But, necktie or no necktie, President Walton forged ahead with Neophogen. The sarcastic barbs of a sophisticated Eastern editor were the least of his troubles as he seemed to be everlastingly busy recruiting students and faculty members. In the latter category, Walton brought a distinguished Polish emigre to Neophogen College in the autumn of 1876. The Gallatin *Tennessean* reported the imminent arrival of Professor Casimir de Zdanowicz in its issue of September 16, 1876:

Prof. Casimir de Zdanowicz is from an old Polish family. He was educated in the Polish college in Paris, followed after the courses of the University of France, where he graduated in science, mathematics, chemistry, etc. After this he entered the School of Mines, where he made rapid progress in Mathematics and Chemistry, after which he was appointed Prof. of Science in the Polish College. He came to the United States in 1870, but remained but a few months, until the war broke out between France and Germany. His sympathies being identified with the country in which he was born, he returned to France and was appointed a commissioned officer in the Engineer corps of the French army and took part in several battles against the German troups. After the war he returned to Paris, and was appointed professor in the Polish College in Paris. During his Professorship he wrote editorials for a French paper, (The Democratii). His political articles against the government and the French Assembly caused him to be prosecuted according to the law against the press and to avoid additional trouble he left France and took the United States as his country of adoption.

Perhaps to provide comic relief from the heavy classical orientation of his faculty, Walton about this time brought Mark Twain to the campus to lecture.[17] Opie Read, a student on the campus when Mark Twain made his visit, years later recalled a post-lecture conversation with the great humorist.

We, the students of the somewhat exaggerated classical institution, Neophogen College, Gallatin, Tennessee, were fondly looking toward the coming of Mark Twain to deliver to us a lecture. President Walton expressed his sensitive concern, "After the lecture you are to sit in a room with the great humorist. I warn you not to light your pipes, for I understand that Mr. Clemens has a contempt for tobacco."

When the thrilling talk had been given, the elder students invited Mark Twain into a small room, "We are going to shut the windows and smoke the humorist out," said one of the leaders.

Soon we began lighting our pipes. After a few moments when some of us began to cough, Mark Twain inquired, "Are you fellows smoking sawdust? Wait a minute, I think I have some regular tobacco."

With that he took from his pocket a big pipe, crumpled off tobacco from a black Kentucky twist and puffed upon us clouds of suffocating smoke.

When we had coughed our way out of the room, we saw Mark Twain silently laughing, as he walked beneath the trees.[18]

A paid insertion in the Gallatin *Examiner*, October 6, 1876, announced the opening of Neophogen for another term. Special mention was made of "scholarships" offered for sale by the school.

---

[17] Traditional stories that circulated in Gallatin told of Twain's appearing unexpectedly at Neophogen and creating such dismay on the part of the president that he locked his guest out of the lecture hall and forced him to speak out of doors.

[18] Opie Read, *Mark Twain and I* (Chicago: Reilly and Lee Co., 1940), p. 9.

Also promoted in the school's catalog, the sale of "scholarships" were in truth methods of achieving advance payment in return for reduction in tuition charges amounting to $50 per year. The advance payment "scholarships" or certificates were transferable —could be sold and purchased—and seemed to be a very doubtful financial device to raise quick cash for the school.

In the offering of "Female Scholarships," advance payment of $1,000 would gain a "scholarship" good for a collegiate education, including tuition, room and board and a very special relationship with the president's family. Walton explained:

> Ten female students will be received into the family of the President of Neophogen College, and trained as his children, boarded, clothed, books and stationary furnished, and graduated in a regular collegiate course for $1,000 each, payable in advance . . . they must not be under 12 years of age and able to read and write. The chief inducement in presenting this is to give the President an opportunity to train remarkable characters to the honor of the College, and to enable him to verify his views in regard to the development of any youth of medium organization, when full control is given and implicit confidence reposed.[19]

However, from the beginning Walton's "scholarships," described in dignified terms and eloquently rationalized, were transparent efforts to get his hands on badly needed cash. But these and other efforts failed and Walton had, by October 7, 1876, fallen in arrears with lease payments to Howard Lodge and had borrowed $600 from John T. Baber to continue operating the school. To secure both debts, Walton made an assignment to Baber first as treasurer of Howard Lodge and secondly as an individual "of any monies due from patrons of me or the school known as Neophogen College which I am conducting in the building." [20] Thus was recorded the beginning of the end of Neophogen College.

But the end was not apparent on the campus where the school year 1876-1877 saw the largest student body that had ever been assembled in Gallatin. Two hundred eighty three young men and

---

[19] Gallatin *Examiner,* October 6, 1876.
[20] *SCR, Deed Book #31,* p. 140.

women completed the course work and found their separate grades for "application, punctuality and deportment" reproduced on the pages of the *Annual Catalog, 1877-78*. Public debate between Neophogen students in April and May had been reported with praise in the local press.[21] Patrons of the college doubtless shared the enthusiasm of the valedictory speaker, student E. M. Cockrell, Jr., who during commencement exercises May 25 paid tribute to President Walton who "can point with pride to many young men who were educated beneath this roof and who are now filling prominent positions in life. Some are found in the pulpit . . . others at the bar . . . some editors . . . others in the recitation halls teaching and training. . . . How gratifying this must be to him who is so worthy of his position as president of Neophogen College. . . . I bespeak for Neophogen College . . . a most brilliant and happy future." [22]

The large enrollment of 1876-1877 seems to have generated funds enough to keep Neophogen alive for another year—its last. The tenor of the catalog for 1877-78, its text largely copied from earlier editions, was as optomistic and confident as ever. The faculty listing continued to be impressive. In addition to President Walton and his wife, there were: Lorenz Rohr, A.M., Munich University, Bavaria, Professor of Latin, Greek and German; Casimir Zdanowicz, A.M., University of France, Paris, Professor of Mathematics; I. J. Morris, A.M., Professor of Grammar; Robert Kidd, A.M., Professor Elocution; A. L. Blackman, B.S., Professor Penmanship, Phonography and Bookkeeping; W. D. Corkran, A.M., Professor of English Literature and Moral Science; S. Athanasiades, A.M., University of Athens, Greece, Professor of Ancient and Modern Greek; C. T. Browne, A.M., Professor and Master, School of Natural Sciences; Mrs. A. A. Walton, M.M., Instructress, Piano, Guitar and Voice Culture; Henry L. Farmer, Professor of Instrumental Music; J. W. Gray, M.D., Professor Hygiene and Medical Jurisprudence; Miss S. C. Coffee, Preceptress; and Mrs. M. B. Foote, Mistress of Cuisine and Hygiene.

---

[21] Gallatin *Examiner,* April 6, May 11, 1877.
[22] *Ibid.,* June 1, 1877.

Prof. Walton also acted as Bursar and Corkran was Secretary of the Faculty. Rohr, Zdanowicz, and Athanasiades were also shown to be teaching in fields other than their primary listings. It was noted that Professor Morris was the author of Morris' *Grammar* and Professor Kidd the author of Kidd's *Elocution*.

Neophogen had a school of law "now thoroughly organized" in 1877. The suggestion that it had not always been thus surely refers to the law school's uncertain beginnings and its meagre patronage. In 1876, only four young men were graduated from the one-year law course.[23] No records of other graduates have been discovered, although there were surely students in the program during 1877-78. Eleven subjects were covered during two five-month terms enabling students to complete the law course during one academic year. There were four members of law school faculty, "men of age and experience, having rare qualifications, and . . . highly distinguished in their profession." They were S. F. Wilson, dean; B. F. Allen, W. S. Munday, and James W. Blackmore. All were actively engaged in the practice of law at Gallatin.[24]

The catalog of 1877-78, the school's last, hints broadly that individual members of the faculty might have been paid on some kind of incentive plan. Under the heading "Individual Enterprise," is printed this statement:

> What is the duty of many is generally neglected by all.
> Here is *continued* and *special* stimulus to President and Professors; here are no easy and assured positions, with fixed and positive salaries, but they depend upon the patronage, prosperity and reputation of the institution.
> That this should be so is too obvious for comment. A very little knowledge of human nature is necessary to see why. To each teacher it is plain; the greater the labor, the greater the reward.

There are no indications that President Walton enjoyed even a small measure of success in his offers to sell lots to "families

---

[23] *Ibid.*, August 11, 1876.
[24] *Neophogen Annual Catalog, 1877-78.* Wilson was an unsuccessful candidate for Governor of Tennessee in 1880.

wishing to purchase and improve" them. His interest in raising a life fund "for the relief of unfortunate literary men" seems never to have proceeded beyond the pages of his catalogs.

Walton's ambitious plans seem generally to have been self-contradictory. He sought to have both the *best* and the *cheapest* college, and to have coeducation of males and females yet isolation of the sexes from each other by stringently enforced rules of decorum. He promised to give special attention to a variety of students' personal needs from feeble health to stammering and stuttering while offering a range of extracurricular activities that could only be maintained by an institution three or four times its size. He professed to specialize—yet his approach was to fire a broadside.

Sometime during 1877-78, the financial difficulties of the times compounded in Walton's glorious dreams for Neophogen College, overtook the intrepid promoter-educator. Unable to make his lease payments to Howard Lodge, Walton abandoned Gallatin in the early summer of 1878 and returned to Cross Plains. The facilities that Walton had occupied were reopened in the fall of the same year under the former name of Howard Female College with W. H. Haynes serving as president.

After returning Neophogen College to Cross Plains, Walton operated it successfully for several years before irreconcilable differences with his partners in ownership forced him out. Soon after he left its administration, the school's name was changed to Cross Plains Normal College. Walton remained in the community and conducted a local private school there for the rest of his life.

Chapter IV

TULLATUSKEE NORMAL COLLEGE

The Tullatuskee Normal College was organized at Bethpage in 1899 by local citizens who raised money sufficient to erect a schoolhouse and who were granted a state charter "to conduct a Normal College, to confer degrees, and to teach any useful profession, trade, or business or art." [1]

The incorporators to whom the charter of the Tullatuskee Normal College was granted were J. B. Hanna, W. F. Moss, Joe Harrell, M. M. Cockreham, and E. A. Woodson, all of Bethpage. Z. T. Key of Bethpage, although not appearing as an incorporator, was also active in promoting the school and raising the initial subscription.

As was often the practice in establishing general welfare corporations of this kind, subscribers to the school fund became stockholders with voting rights to select the directors of the organization. For Tullatuskee Normal College there were forty-three original stockholders whose individual subscriptions ranged in amounts from $5 to $200. [2]

A brief announcement of the opening session of the Normal College, printed in the Gallatin *Semi-Weekly News,* October 14, 1899, stated that Professor E. B. Wilson was in charge of the school and Miss Pattie Malone and A. J. Hibbett were the other faculty members. Tullatuskee was recommended as "a good school for teachers and those preparing to teach."

After the opening of the college, little of its activity seems to have been either publicly or privately recorded. Such information as is available about Tullatuskee's first decade is drawn from the incomplete files of Gallatin newspapers of the period.

Three years after Wilson opened the school, a newspaper reference to Tullatuskee appeared in the *Semi-Weekly News.* In its

---

[1] *SCR, Deed Book #46,* p. 410.
[2] *Minutes of Board of Education of Tullatuskee Normal School at Bethpage,* Private Collection of Mrs. Virginia Key Wemyss.

edition of August 2, 1902, the *News* revealed that E. B. Wilson had been replaced and that G. O. Mudge was serving as principal. The new principal made this announcement:

Tullatuskee Normal
College
Fall Term opens
Monday, Aug. 4, 1902
Better equipped than ever. If you wish your boy or girl to attend school in a quiet, moral healthful community; a school in which the teachers are personally interested in the development of a high type of manhood or womanhood, write for information and terms.
G. O. MUDGE, *Prin.*,
Bethpage, Tenn.

In a brief notice of the end of the school year in May, 1905, it was reported that "Prof. Sisk, principal of Tullatuskee Normal, has been re-elected." [3] However, Sisk must have resigned during the summer as the Nashville *Banner* of July 31 announced that R. L. Smith "of Louisiana" had been selected as the new principal for the school and a Miss Eva Williamson had been made Smith's assistant. Approximately 100 students were enrolled for the term beginning August 1, 1905. J. Woodall Murrey of Gallatin was principal in 1907 and 1908. In 1909 E. B. Wilson returned as principal and needed only one other teacher—Miss Nettie Woodson—to assist him at the school.

Funds for the operating budget, which consisted almost entirely of salaries for the teachers, were supplied from tuition charges. In its beginning years, Tullatuskee's revenues were boosted by tuitions paid by its boarding students who had been attracted from surrounding communities by the prospects of earning a normal college degree. But these sources of income seem to have been lost in less than a decade. At the commencement exercises May 21, 1908, only five students were graduated[4] and

---

[3] Gallatin *News,* May 27, 1905.

[4] *Tullatuskee Commencement Program, May 21, 1908,* Private Collection of Kenneth Thomson.

shortly thereafter all pretense of being a degree-conferring institution was dropped.

When the stockholders' annual meeting was held in 1908, it was acknowledged that school records for the period 1899-1908—the normal college's brief life span—had been lost.[5] It is supposed that Tullatuskee, like so many of its contemporary institutions, was launched with an emotional enthusiasm that its financial resources could not sustain.

Minutes of the annual meeting of the "Board of Education of the Tullatuskee Normal School at Bethpage" from 1909 to 1923 have been preserved and indicate that during this period the school became assimilated into the county school system. The trustees of the original Tullatuskee Normal College held title to the property until 1923 when they conveyed it to the county of Sumner.

The printing of the commencement program of 1908 seems to have been the last occasion on which the school was identified by its chartered name: Tullatuskee Normal College.

Who suggested this unusual name? What were its origins? What does it mean?

While it is not known who suggested it, the name Tullatuskee was taken from an Indian word meaning the waving corn blade which was symbolic of perpetual motion. This is the name said to have been given by the Indians to Isaac Bledsoe, early hunter and explorer of Sumner County who discovered Bledsoe's Lick and later settled and built a fort there in 1784.

---

[5] *Minutes of Board of Education of Tullatuskee Normal School at Bethpage.*

CHAPTER V

ISAAC FRANKLIN INSTITUTE

DREAMS OF a financially self-sustaining educational institution at Gallatin seemed about to be answered in 1846 through the unexpected death of Isaac Franklin of Sumner County whose last will and testament was found to provide approximately $600,000 from his estate to create and endow the Isaac Franklin Institute. His will directed that the campus and buildings be situated on his beautiful Fairvue plantation two miles west of Gallatin on lands lying directly across the highway from the present site of Volunteer State Community College.

It is generally believed that the gift provided by Franklin's will was the first substantial endowment of an institution of learning in the state of Tennessee. At the very least, the Nashville *Banner* observed of Franklin on November 30, 1912, "He deserves to be remembered as the first native Tennessean . . . who provided out of his fortune for the establishment and maintenance of an educational institution."

The potential impact of Franklin's bequest was enormous when compared with Cornelius Vanderbilt's first endowment gift of $500,000 to Vanderbilt University made thirty years later. Franklin's generosity and purpose, however, were thwarted when his will was contested and a later court ruling held the bequest invalid.

Born in Sumner County May 26, 1789, the son of pioneers James and Mary Lauderdale Franklin, Isaac had early participated with his older brothers in the barge trade to Natchez and New Orleans. By the late 1820's he was engaged in buying and selling slaves in New Orleans; and from 1830 to 1836, he and his partner, John Armfield, were regarded as the leading slave traders in the South.[1] During this time Franklin amassed extensive plantation

---

[1] Frederic Bancroft, *Slave Trading in the Old South* (Baltimore: J. H. Furst Co., 1931), p. 58.

lands in Louisiana and owned at one time approximately 2,000 acres in Sumner County.

The value of the endowment that Franklin had established could not be determined until after the executors had appraised his estate. While he had declared in his will that the primary purpose of the school or "seminary" was to educate his own children, his nieces and nephews, and their descendants. Franklin had also provided that, should the endowment be sufficient, "the poor children" of Sumner County should also be educated and supported at the seminary. When an inventory of the estate was made, it was determined that the value of the endowment was approximately $600,000 and thus sufficiently large to provide education for large numbers of young people outside the Franklin family.

Designating his brothers, James and William, as the first trustees of the endowment fund, Franklin had outlined their duties and set forth his general plan for the school in his will. He directed that the monies

> . . . be laid out in building proper and suitable edifices on my said Fairvue plantation in the County of Sumner and State of Tennessee, for an academy or seminary, the furnishing the same with fixtures and furniture, and the employment of such teachers and professors, male and female, as may be considered necessary by my said trustees, for the education, board, and clothing of the children of my brothers and sisters, and their descendants, as well as my own children, and their descendants, in the best and most suitable and proper manner for American youths, having a particular regard to a substantial and good English education, and such other higher and ornamental branches as the aforesaid revenues, &c., will enable my said trustees to accomplish; and if the revenues, &c., should be sufficient therefor, I also wish that the poor children in said County of Sumner, of unexceptionable character, and such as my said trustees may select, should likewise be educated and supported during the time at the same seminary; and after the death of my aforesaid brothers, it is my will and desire that the aforesaid trust shall be continued and pass over forever in the heirs of my said brothers, to pass the estate, and that the magistrates of the County Court of said County of Sumner and State of Tennessee, and their successors in office, be thereafter

77

the perpetual superintendents of the aforesaid seminary, to see that my intentions be fully carried into effect.

Franklin's generosity was hailed by the Nashville *Whig* September 12, 1846, who found his provision for the education of poor children especially laudatory:

> The main object in the nature of events, here designed by the testator, namely, a provision for the *poor children* of Sumner county, is modestly cloaked under a provision seeming to be chiefly for his own brothers' and sisters' posterity. This noble benevolence effectually extracts the sting of poverty and orphanage in Sumner county, and makes blessed a lot usually so mournful, and so exciting our sympathies. A life of strenuous and laborious exertion in the pursuit of wealth, and crowned with extraordinary success, is worthily ended by the devotion of its hordes to such a truly glorious and Christian benevolence, and is forever embalmed in the memory of men, and snatched from the oblivion that so soon shroud the names of ordinary mortals.

A charter was granted to Isaac Franklin Institute on December 1, 1847, by act of the Tennessee legislature. A "succession of five hundred years" was provided as were "a seal, authority to make statutes for its regulation, the same power of conferring degrees as is possessed by any literary institution in the State, the faculty of suing and being sued . . . and the power of acquiring and holding, for the purpose of its creation, property real and personal." And, as was typical of such charters in this period, it was provided that both faculty and students would be exempt from militia duty and jury service.[2]

Early in 1848 Franklin's widow, Adelicia Hayes Franklin, sold the interest that she and her daughter Emma had in the Fairvue plantation to trustee William Franklin for the avowed purpose of expediting the organization and opening of the institute. A year later Mrs. Franklin, who was already questioning the legacies provided in the will, was married to Joseph A. S. Acklen of Nashville. Seeking formal legal approval of their plans to activate the school, the trustees filed a petition in the Seventh District

---

[2] *Tennessee Acts, 1847-1848*, Chapter VI, pp. 24-28.

Court, West Feliciana, Louisiana, "to carry the will of Isaac Franklin into execution." [3] The widow Franklin, now Mrs. Acklen, contested the petition of the trustees and joined a legal struggle that was not finally concluded until June, 1852, when the Louisiana Supreme Court ruled that the provision of Franklin's will for the creation and endowment of a school out of revenues derived in part from property and plantation operations in Louisiana was "void on the grounds that it set up a perpetuity." [4]

The litigation had been long and costly—especially to the "poor children" of Sumner County whose immediate prospects for schooling were hopelessly scuttled. The school was not lost until concerted efforts to save it had been beaten down in court. The people of Sumner County rallied to the side of the trustees of Isaac Franklin Institute but to no avail. No one fought longer nor harder to save the institute than Isaac Franklin's brothers and nephews in Sumner County. Their efforts to sustain the will and preserve the institute are shown in detail in the Louisiana district court records of the litigation compiled under the title *Succession of Isaac Franklin* and printed and bound in 918 pages.[5]

---

[3] *Succession of Isaac Franklin,* Seventh Judicial District Court, West Feliciana, Louisiana, circa 1852, p. 910.

[4] 7 Louisiana Ann. 395, 1852. This decision upheld the lower court ruling of Judge James S. Sterling of the Seventh Judicial District of Louisiana made June 28, 1851. *Succession of Isaac Franklin,* p. 266.

[5] Over the signature of Charles B. Collins, Clerk, Seventh Judicial District Court, West Feliciana, Louisiana, the *Succession of Isaac Franklin* is certified to be "a full, true and complete transcript of all the proceedings had, evidence adduced and used . . . and documents of record and file . . . in the matter of Mrs. Adelicia Acklen . . . et als., opposing petition of trustees of Isaac Franklin Institute, to carry will of Isaac Franklin into execution."

CHAPTER VI

PYTHIAN COLLEGE

SURELY THE MOST GRANDIOSE PLANS ever formulated for a private institution of higher learning in Sumner County were developed in the early 1890's by Rowena Lodge of the fraternal order Knights of Pythias at Gallatin. A building committee from the lodge acquired a site of thirty acres, retained an architect to plan the campus and its buildings, and dedicated a gigantic cornerstone for its first structure with impressive ceremony on May 2, 1894. The occasion attracted widespread attention and was hailed with approbation by newspapers throughout the state. However, a short time thereafter the ambitious venture known as the Pythian College failed, a victim of the financial panic of 1893-1895.[1]

What were the origins of the movement to develop the Pythian College at Gallatin? Who were the people who furnished the impetus to the project? What were the circumstances of its failure? The answer to these questions can be constructed from the surviving sketchy minutes of Rowena Lodge, newspaper accounts and court records of the period, and an understanding of the community in which the school was to have been located.

In 1890, Gallatin, the county seat of Sumner County, had a population of just over 3,000 persons. Its earliest settlers had brought with them an abiding interest in education with the result that schools and academies had flourished in the area since Indian days. Prominently located on East Main Street near the public square was Howard Female College, a property of the local lodge of the Independent Order of Odd Fellows since 1857. While the Howard Lodge I.O.O.F. had operated Howard College by leasing it to a president or principal, the operation had, on the whole, been a successful one and perhaps, in the minds of some of the Knights of Pythias, worthy of imitation. It was, at

---

[1] Times were so hard that the opening of the Tennessee State Centennial Exposition originally scheduled for 1896 was delayed a year to provide time to get its finances in order.

least, proof that a fraternal order could be a sponsoring force in education; and doubtless at a lodge meeting in 1890 or 1891, the possibility of building a Pythian College or University was first discussed.[2]

The first acknowledged interest of Rowena Lodge in developing a college is revealed in a deed dated July 16, 1891, by which trustees of the Gallatin Male Seminary conveyed their school lot to the lodge for use as a site for "a Pythian College." The tract was located on the north side of West Main Street, and was bounded on the east by the C&N Railroad, on the north by the L&N Railroad main line, and on the west by the property of W. T. Dale. It included the present location of the Kraft Foods plant and other adjoining properties to the west and north.[3] One cannot escape the impression that the trustees of Gallatin Male Seminary were following the same route taken some 35 years earlier by the trustees of Sumner Female Institute when they abandoned the plant and campus of their financially distraught institution to Howard Lodge No. 13, I.O.O.F. In both cases the gift of property was made on the condition that it be used for educational purposes.

With the old Gallatin Male Seminary property in hand, Rowena Lodge designated three incorporators and the Grand Lodge appointed two to apply for a state charter for the Pythian College. In response to their application, a charter of incorporation was awarded by the State of Tennessee July 20, 1891. The charter set forth plans for the new college in detail and outlined the relationship between it and the state and national orders of the Knights of Pythias:

> State of Tennessee.   Charter of Incorporation.
> Be it known that C. H. Sanders, J. H. Lightfoot, Geo. E. Seay, J. B. Howison, and Jas. W. Blackmore and their successors, are hereby constituted a body politic and corporate of the name and style of the
> "Pythian College"
> the same to be located in or near the town of Gallatin, Sumner

---

[2] No minutes of these years are known to have been preserved.
[3] *SCR, Deed Book #41*, p. 171.

County, Tennessee, and conducted under the patronage, care and supervision of the Order of the Knights of Pythias of the World, acting through its Subordinate Lodge at Gallatin, Tennessee, its Grand Lodge of the State, and its Supreme Lodge, in conformity to Law and its usages, and in compliance with the terms and conditions attached to the donation or gift of what is known as the Gallatin Male Seminary and its properties to said Order, or the Subordinate Lodge thereof, at Gallatin, Tennessee, for the organization of an Institution of Learning—

The general purposes for which this charter is sought and granted is the establishment, endowment, development of a college, or university, for the education of the youth of the land: And to this end through an executive committee, executive council, board of visitors, or such administrative agencies or officers as it may elect, appoint or select, consistently with law, and the relation it sustains to the Order of the Knights of Pythias, and Rowena Lodge thereof, under the terms of the gift accepted by the latter and ratified by the Grand Lodge Knights of Pythias of the State, establish a curriculum of studies, fix the terms and conditions of matriculation and graduation therein and from time to time make such changes in reference thereto as wisdom experience and the requirements of the institution demand consistent with law. It is authorized and empowered to confer degrees, grant diplomas, establish departments and special courses of study, erect chapels, dormitories, Lyceums, recitation and all other room and buildings needed and a gymnasium. It is also authorized and empowered to purchase, receive by gift, devise or otherwise all real estate that may be needed for the purposes of the institution. It may also receive by gift, bequest, donation, or otherwise money, school apparatus and all other kinds of personal property that may be used or converted into uses available to develop the institution. It may take real estate or other property in payment or part payment of debts due the corporation and dispose of the same for its use and benefit. The further general power of the corporation shall be to sue and be sued by the corporate name: to have and use a common seal which it may alter at pleasure, and if it have no common seal then the signature of the name of the corporation by any duly authorized official, or officials shall be legal and binding. It shall also have power to establish bylaws and make all needed rules and regulations, not in consistent with law, for the government and operation of the institution. The active control and management of said institution and its affairs shall be vested in an executive committee of five to be appointed by the Grand

Lodge of the State, and Rowena Lodge, a subordinate Lodge of the Knights of Pythias at Gallatin, Tennessee, in the proportion provided in the contract and agreement accepted and adopted by said Rowena Lodge and ratified by the Grand Lodge Knights of Pythias of the State, providing for the college herein chartered.

The terms and tenure of office of said Executive Committee shall be as provided by the parties empowered to select same and in conformity to the laws of the State, and the number of said committee may be increased hereafter if all parties interested under the contract ratified by the Grand Lodge Knights of Pythias of the state so agree. But all members of said Executive Committee shall always be Knights of Pythias in good standing in the order, and if any member thereof cease to be such his position in and as a member of said Executive Committee shall thereby become vacated and the same supplied by the branch of said Order entitled to fill the place of the member so vacating said membership on said Executive Committee.

The said Order of Knights of Pythias may from Rowena Lodge at Gallatin, Tennessee, from the Grand Lodge of Tennessee, and from the Supreme Lodge of the Order create a Board of Visitors, which shall have a general visitorial and supervising jurisdiction and watch over the general educational policy of the Institution. The Executive Committee shall render accounts properly itemized and verified of all receipts, disbursements and contracts made, received and acted upon by them, and shall keep true and accurate minutes of all their transactions affecting the funds and interests of the Institution. Their accounts shall be rendered to Rowena Lodge Knights of Pythias at Gallatin, Tennessee and Grand Lodge Knights of Pythias of Tennessee, and, if called for, to the Supreme Lodge Knights of Pythias of the World.

The Board of visitors provided for shall be members of the Order of Knights of Pythias in good standing, but shall have no power to manage, direct or control said institution. A purely honorary board of visitors composed of eminent Knights of Pythias and others interested in education may also be created.

The Executive Committee provided for shall keep a record of their proceedings which shall at all times be open to the inspection of Rowena Lodge Knights of Pythias or a committee therefrom or to any committee from the Grand or Supreme Lodge of said Order: And for the purpose of keeping and verifying its record said Executive Committee may elect one of its members President and one Secretary and Treasurer: and all contracts made by the same shall be signed by these officials. The general welfare of society, not individual profit is to be the object for which this charter is granted and hence the members are not stockholders in the legal sense of the term, and no dividend or profits shall be divided among the members. We the undersigned apply to the State of Tennessee by virtue of the laws of the land for a charter of incorporation for the purposes and with the power etc. declared in the foregoing instruments.

Witness our hands the 16th day of July, 1891. George E. Seay, J. B. Howison, Jas. W. Blackmore, C. H. Sanders, J. H. Lightfoot.

By the autumn of 1891, Rowena Lodge had decided to renew the operation of the boys school formerly known as Gallatin Male Seminary. Under Rowena Lodge's sponsorship it was called simply "a Pythian school for boys" and was maintained in operation until after the turn of the century.[4]

During this same time, the incorporators of Pythian College apparently concluded that the Male Seminary tract of eight acres was not large enough for their campus. Consequently, a new location for the college was chosen. Two parcels of land containing a combined total of 25 acres and lying on the west side of North Water Street one mile north of the public square were purchased by the college executive committee. The location was bounded on the north by Douglas Pike, on the west by the L&N Railroad main line and on the south by lands of James J. Turner.[5]

From early in its consideration of a Pythian College at Gallatin, Rowena Lodge had counted on the support of the Grand[6] and Supreme[7] Lodges. While no specific agreements for Supreme Lodge participation in the Pythian College had been reached by early 1894, the executive committee pushed ahead with plans to lay the cornerstone for the main building. The date of May 2, 1894, was selected for this ceremonial occasion and what a day it must have been!

The date was selected to coincide with the opening of the annual session of the Grand Lodge of Tennessee which was meet-

---

[4] *Journal of Proceedings, Supreme Lodge Knights of Pythias, Volume VIII* (1894), p. 6866.

[5] *SCR, Deed Book #43*, p. 40.

[6] State.

[7] International.

ing in Nashville May 2 and 3. The cornerstone ceremonies were scheduled to be held in the afternoon of the first day after the business session had been adjourned in Nashville and Grand Lodge officers and delegates had been taken to Gallatin by special train.

The Nashville Banner, in its edition of May 3, described the colorful pageantry that attended the departure from Nashville:

> . . . The great majority of the members set out for the Union depot, where a special train of eight coaches waited to take them to Gallatin . . . the local divisions of Uniform Rank . . . were mustering at their armory on the corner of Summer and Union streets. Headed by the Phillips and Buttorf Band, a hundred brilliantly trapped and helmeted Knights moved up Summer to Church and down Church to the Union depot . . . with probably 600 people on board the train moved out at 12 o'clock.

The train arrived at the campus site about one mile north of the Gallatin depot in less than an hour and its passengers were greeted by the massed membership of Rowena Lodge, its local Uniform Division and a large assemblage of townspeople. A brief address of welcome was given by Mayor George N. Guthrie who then adjourned the meeting for mid-day "dinner" served by the local Pythian ladies. The food was well received by the *Banner* reporter who wrote:

> The dinner was all that a dinner of its kind could be, crisp barbecued meat, fresh pies, airy cakes and ices made a repast to be remembered. . . . There was plenty of everything.

After "dinner" the crowd settled itself for the speeches by which the cornerstone dedication would be accomplished. The principal speaker was Fred E. Wheaton, Grand Chancellor of the Minnesota Grand Lodge, Knights of Pythias, and he lost no time in establishing the importance of the occasion:

> We have gathered here today under the tri-color of the Knights of Pythias for the purpose of planting in the soil of Tennessee a corner stone which is to mark the central spot from which shall radiate the great Pythian educational movement. This movement is not confined to this county, nor to this state, nor to this country, but to the order universal. The eyes of the Pythian world are

today turned toward Gallatin to witness the inauguration of a movement that is the most potent evidence of the progress and development of the order of Knights of Pythias. This comparatively young fraternity has allied itself with the growth and development of this great country in which we live.

Much good has already been done in this line by the Knights of Pythias . . . but it remained for Rowena Lodge, Gallatin and Tennessee to urge upon the order universal the necessity of founding this university, which promises to be the greatest thing that has yet been done by Pythians. . . .

To the city and people of Gallatin I have to say that whatever energy, time and money you may have already expended in this enterprise, if you are tired of your contract, Minnesota stands ready and willing to take it off your hands. Hereafter Gallatin will be looked on by Knights of Pythias of the world at large as the head of this great order and a centre of education and refinement.[8]

Other speakers[9] joined in the congratulations to Gallatin and Tennessee for promoting the Pythian University and for winning Supreme Lodge support in making it a project of Pythians everywhere. The *Banner* observed:

Such an institution would be an ornament and a benefit to any community and the fact that it comes to the South, Tennessee and Gallatin speaks volumes for the energy and influence of the Knights of this state. With such an institution established on her soil Tennessee will naturally be given an additional prominence in the thought and interest of the great and growing order.

The huge limestone cornerstone, approximately 4' x 4' x 6' in size, was reported in place by Jules G. Zwicker, a Nashville architect who designed the building whose corner was thus marked. The cornerstone was supplied from a quarry near Bowling Green, Kentucky. It was delivered to the site by the L&N Railroad which built a temporary spur track 400 feet long from its main line to the designated spot for the stone. After a sealed box containing the usual papers of historical interest had been

---

[8] Nashville *Banner*, May 3, 1894.

[9] Brig. Gen. Alex Allison of Knoxville, formerly of Sumner County; W. B. Holmes, Lebanon; W. P. Griffin, Grand Chancellor; and Col. H. White Hall, financial agent for the college.

placed within the stone, a ritual of dedication was conducted and a brief concluding address was given. The ceremonies were then adjourned and the crowd turned toward town, following in the line of march taken up by the Knights of the Uniform Rank. The procession was greeted warmly by the citizens who waved and cheered from the sidewalks and houses along the way. By the end of the day most of the out-of-town guests were en route back to Nashville on the special train that had brought them to Gallatin for the afternoon's festivities. A few, however, remained in Gallatin overnight to attend the ball given in the evening at the Tompkins Opera House.[10]

Throughout Tennessee there was interest registered in what was happening at Gallatin. The new Pythian institution had been hailed on May 1 by the Chattanooga *Press:*

> Tomorrow morning at Nashville the meeting of the Grand Lodge . . . will take place, and in the afternoon the delegates will go to Gallatin to lay the corner stone of the Pythians University, one of the first Pythian institutions of learning in the world.

In West Tennessee readers of the Memphis *Appeal-Avalanche* found this account of the events of May 2 in Gallatin:

> At Gallatin this afternoon the cornerstone of the only Pythian university in the world was laid in the presence of 4,000 people. The Grand Lodge from Nashville was met at the train by the local lodge and escorted to the grounds. . . .
> This is the only educational institution in the world to which the Supreme Lodge has given the right to use the word Pythian. Thirty acres of ground have been purchased and $100,000 will be expended on buildings.[11]

When the supply of superlatives used to describe the events surrounding the cornerstone dedication became exhausted, the editors of the *Banner* turned to a description of the main building, aided by a three-column reproduction of the architect's rendering of it. The building as illustrated was larger than any structure on Vanderbilt University campus at Nashville. In fact, its elaborate design overshadowed every public building in Middle

---

[10] Nashville *Banner,* May 3, 1894.
[11] Memphis *Appeal-Avalanche,* May 3, 1894.

Tennessee with the possible exception of the State Capitol at Nashville. It is no surprise that the *Banner* reported that architect Jules G. Zwicker contemplated "a building of elaborate proportions and costly design. Its cost will be between $150,000 and $200,000."

That a monumental structure was envisioned is clearly revealed in the *Banner's* eight-paragraph description of the "Main Building of the Pythian University."

The building will be 357 feet long and 100 feet deep through the side wings and 150 feet deep in the centre. It will be constructed so as to be perfectly fire-proof, and the outside will be faced with stone, probably from Bowling Green, like the corner-stone. A basement 12 feet deep will extend under the entire building. The first, second and third floor will be 15 feet clear of floor and ceiling. The main entrance will be a vestibule entering into a portico which will introduce you into the rotunda. This rotunda will be octagon in shape and extend through the three stories, being lighted by a large round skylight at the top centre.

From the rotunda will extend two corridors the entire length of the building. The rotunda and corridors are to be floored with tiling. A stairway of iron and marble will be on each side of the rotunda.

The vestibule and rotunda will be wainscotted with marble four feet high. The toilet-rooms and lavatories on each floor will be of marble and tiling.

To the left of the entrance will be the private rooms of the Chancellor and the reception-rooms. On the right will be the offices of the Secretary and Treasurer, with fire-proof walls, behind which will be the faculty and trustees' rooms. In the rear will be the gymnasium which will extend from the basement below up through the first floor and have a gallery. On each floor there will be two cloak-rooms and lavatories. The other rooms in the first floor will be devoted to civil engineering and literature, two professors' rooms and a ladies toilet. There will be two rear exits.

Over the vestibule on the second floor will be the library and reading-room, which will extend to the roof and have a gallery on three sides. Over the gymnasium will be the chapel, which will also reach through two stories with galleries on two sides. On this floor will also be rooms for the commercial and natural science departments and the zoological and botanical museums.

On the third floor will be the law, chemical, and physical departments with Lecture rooms, laboratories and a geological museum. A stairway will lead up to the roof which will extend around the circular skylight and be protected by a railing.

In the basement there will be workshops for the mechanical and electrical engineers and rooms for metal and cement tests and a hydraulic and metallurgical laboratory and applied chemistry. There will also be storerooms for instruments and the janitors' living rooms.

The style of the structure, as may be seen from the accompanying picture will be classic Roman with columns and pilasters. The main entrance will consist of three arched doorways with tablets on each side for the inscriptions and a balcony above. The gable will be relieved with a Pythian emblem and under the frieze will appear in large letters, "Pythian University."

The second story windows will have tablets under them, each bearing the name of someone famous as a scientist or a scholar. The main entrance will be emphasized by a portico and the side entrance by four columns. All the way around the building will be crowned by a balustrade, with vases at intervals showing plumes.[12]

In a letter to the Nashville *Banner*, H. E. Truex, president of the executive committee of the college, took exception to the size and cost of the building as stated in that newspaper on May 3. He explained that no plan would be "finally accepted until it was demonstrated . . . that the specifications could be materialized within the . . . limit of $100,000. . . . The building will not cost anywhere near $150,000. There still needs books and brains to equip this monumental centre of friendship, charity and benevolence." [13]

Truex wrote, "The building is to be 257 feet front and not 357. No contracts have as yet been given out, and no one can tell where the stone is to come from . . . at any rate, we propose to go right on as rapidly as can be done, and not stop or halt until the shadow of the Pythian flag falls through the crowning dome upon the tiling in the rotunda below." [14]

Almost lost in the excitement of May 2 was the brief appear-

---

[12] Nashville *Banner*, May 3, 1894.

[13] The order's motto: Friendship, Charity and Benevolence usually abbreviated F.C.&B.

[14] Nashville *Banner*, May 4, 1894.

ance on the speaker's platform of Col. H. White Hall, the financial agent and fund raiser for the college. Calling on the people of Gallatin and Sumner County for liberal contributions to the college fund, Col. Hall announced that subscription books would be opened to local donors the same day. Subscriptions could be made at the Mechanics Bank and at Schell's Drug Store. Two years later the failure of substantial local contributions to materialize would be cited as one of the principal reasons for abandonment of the entire project by the Supreme Lodge.

During the course of the local subscription drive silver spoons, the bowls embossed with a rendering of the Pythian University main building, were sold to raise money for the school. In addition to the rendering, the spoons bore the inscription "Pythian University, Gallatin, Tennessee." It is supposed that sales of the embossed spoons were promoted by W. F. Roth, prominent local jeweler and member of the college executive committee.

Soon after the May 4 ceremonies at Gallatin, White Hall, director of fund raising for the university, apparently visited Pythian Lodges throughout Tennessee. At Chattanooga he addressed Damon Lodge No. 2 sometime in July. The meeting was reported in *The Weekly Pythian Period,* July 25, 1894:

> Brother White Hall paid us a visit in the interest of the Pythian College at Gallatin, and gave us a most interesting talk on that interesting subject. In fact, he talked so well that in the language of the poet 'we came across' and made his heart happy. Our college, though, should not need much talking up, for it should be the pride of every Pythian . . . and ought to be aided in every way without much solicitation.[15]

The Pythian University project was brought to the attention of the universal order of the brotherhood during its biennial convention in Washington, D.C., in early September, 1894. The incorporators of the school offered to convey the institution complete with all of its properties to the Supreme Lodge provided that it always be used for purposes of education. A special committee, appointed to determine "what steps, if any, this Supreme

---

[15] *The Weekly Pythian Period* was the news organ of the Grand Lodge of Tennessee and was published at Nashville.

body.should take to aid in developing and effecting its usefulness," made a comprehensive report on the status of the university and concluded by recommending that "the tender of Pythian University, located at Gallatin, Tennessee, with its properties, moneys and franchises, be accepted by this body." [16]

The report of the special committee stated that the value of the properties of the university plus the moneys contributed to it amounted to approximately $50,000. It noted that "this body donated $1,000 at its session held in Milwaukee," that contributions of $5,000 and $1,000 had been received from the Grand Lodge of Tennessee and the Rowena Lodge at Gallatin, and that "subordinate lodges in Tennessee, individual Pythians of Gallatin and vicinity and the citizens of Tennessee" had given the remainder.[17]

Midway in the report a romantic description of the Gallatin area and its people was provided:

> The author of creation . . . never made a fairer or better country than that. . . . It is about midway between the north and the south. Heat and cold are never excessive. Its climatic and atmospheric conditions are as fine as can be found in the union . . . the glad music of health is heard in its bubbling streams and on its happy breezes. Its people are moral and tolerant, refined and cultivated. . . . The people are thoroughly permeated with Pythianism and its aims, and they look with loving and hoping eye to this Supreme body to take this institution—the first of this character projected by the order—and develop it into a great university.[18]

Turning its attention to specific legal and administrative details involved in accepting the university as a property of the Supreme body, the committee recommended that the offer be accepted "upon the condition that the title thereto be legally vested in this body for the order, or in some appropriate committees or trustees for the uses and educational ends thereof." The report was continued: "We recommend that the Supreme Chancellor be authorized to appoint a board of regents of six, selected from this body

---

[16] *Journal of Proceedings, Supreme Lodge Knights of Pythias, Volume VIII* (1894) , pp. 6865-6867.
[17] *Ibid.*
[18] *Ibid.*

. . . in whom shall be vested . . . the power to make all contracts and regulations necessary to put the university on foot and keep it in active operation.[19]

To create a fund to put the university in operation, the committee suggested that "a contribution of ten cents be required of each member of the order, payable within the next two years. This . . . should be directly collected by this Supreme Lodge . . . and turned over to the board of regents to be by them expended in attaining the ends embraced in the creation of the institution." [20] Such an assessment would have raised approximately $50,000.

Affirming the enthusiasm with which their recommendations had been made, members of the special committee concluded their report with optimism. "This committee is thoroughly imbued with the belief that if what is herein recommended be adopted by the Supreme Lodge, the university will be an accomplished fact within the next two years, and that in six years it will be the brightest and most precious jewel in the crown of Pythian accomplishments. We feel sure that . . . the university will plant itself firmly in the heart of the order, and thence on its growth and usefulness will be healthful and unimpeded, and that it will greatly redound to the glory of our brother Lord." [21]

On September 8, 1894, the committee report was adopted with two amendments that eliminated the certain financial aid that would have come with the modest but important assessment originally provided and instead "requested" that individual Knights voluntarily contribute to the college fund. With the nation in the throes of a financial panic, it was inevitable that the "request" for contributions from individual Knights was largely ignored.

Two years later the Grand Lodge, meeting at Cleveland, Ohio, found the Pythian University stalled for lack of funds; and after reviewing the conditions of their commitment to it, voted to terminate their projected sponsorship of it. The Lodge acted after

---

[19] *Ibid.*
[20] *Ibid.*
[21] *Ibid.*

receiving a report from a special committee analyzing the plight of the school. It was found that the "requested" contributions had not materialized and, indeed, that no funds had been given from any source within the two years. The entire project seems to have lain dormant. The committee reported: "We find that the board of regents have not assumed any authority, nor taken any steps toward the discharge of their supposed duties, and that all matters connected with said university are practically in the same condition they were prior to the contemplated transfer of title to the Supreme Lodge Knights of Pythias; in fact, the title has not passed either to the Supreme Lodge or to the board of regents, and no responsibility has been accepted or assumed by them." [22]

The committe estimated that "a fund of at least a half million dollars" would be required "to complete and properly equip the buildings and other appointments contemplated by the projectors of this undertaking." Thus it was belatedly realized that the Pythian University was a dream too large to become true. An assessment of the members of the order in such an amount was "deemed unwise" and the university was "allowed to remain in the hands of its original projectors." [23]

Even before the sounding of the death knell by the Supreme Lodge in September, 1896, the Pythian University was in trouble at home. The Grand Chancellor of the Grand Lodge of Tennessee in October, 1894, had declined to authorize the executive committee to turn over the Pythian University to the Supreme Lodge. A brief statement of the Grand Chancellor's belief that he had no authority in the matter was made a part of his report to the Knights of Pythias convention at Chattanooga in early May, 1895:

> On October 10 I received, through Grand Keeper of Records and Seal White, a request from H. E. Truex, president, and W. F. Roth, secretary of the executive committee of the Pythian University, at Gallatin asking that I, as grand Chancellor, authorize said executive committee to turn over the University, its franchises, properties, monies, etc. to the supreme lodge for educational

[22] *Journal of Proceedings, Supreme Lodge Knights of Pythias, Volume IX* (1896), p. 7425.
[23] *Ibid.*

purposes, in accordance with the provisions of the legislation of the supreme lodge at its Washington convention.

With the assistance of Past Grand Chancellor T. C. Lattimore, attorney at law, I investigated the matter, and failing to find any constitutional or legal authority, vesting in me such rights, and believing the grand lodge had no legal nor constitutional interest in the university, I declined to comply with the request of the committee.[24]

In May of 1896 Jules G. Zwicker, architect for the university, had won a judgment in the sum of $2,250 plus interest and court costs against its executive committee. Zwicker had not been paid for his services but found relief in the Chancery Court of Sumner County December 16, 1896, when the Clerk and Master was ordered to sell the properties at public auction if the judgment had not been paid by May, 1897.[25]

Zwicker's judgment was largely satisfied when the Clerk and Master sold the three tracts at public auction May 29, 1897. James W. Blackmore was high bidder for the North Water campus at $1,600 and Thomas L. Buckingham offered the high bid of $600 on the old Male Seminary property.[26] However, Zwicker was back in Chancery Court December 17 and won a decree directing the Clerk and Master to sell a typewriter and table belonging to the executive committee to pay the balance due on his initial judgment after the land sale proceeds had been applied.[27]

The Chancery Court sale of the Male Seminary property seems to have subjected Rowena Lodge to much local criticism. On the day after the sale a committee of the lodge was appointed to investigate possible courses of action and a report was heard a week later. Pointing out that the Male Seminary had been given to Rowena Lodge in trust to be operated as a place of learning, the committee recommended that the lodge authorize its representatives to raise the bid, then still open in Chancery Court, and buy it back.[28] The bid was raised to $650 and notes for its pur-

---

[24] Chattanooga *Daily Times,* May 9, 1895.

[25] *SCR, Chancery Minute Book #17,* pp. 490-492.

[26] *SCR, Chancery Minute Book #18,* p. 114.

[27] *Ibid.,* pp. 251-258.

[28] *Rowena Lodge Minute Book, 1896-1900,* UDC Collection, Clark Chapter, Gallatin, Tenn., June 4, 1897.

chase were signed by the individual members of the committee until such time as the lodge could sell certain stocks it held in a savings and loan association.[29] With the West Main property under its control again, Rowena Lodge on June 25, 1897, appointed trustees to hire a teacher and reopen the boys school.[30]

The Pythian College debacle had left Rowena Lodge understandably self-conscious of its responsibilities in the area of education. One result was that the lodge held tenaciously to its boys school property. Between 1899 and 1901, trustees for the school investigated construction of a residence for the principal to be located on the school grounds. A bid of $1,500 for a suitable house was offered May 18, 1900, and a committee set about to raise the money. Their efforts seem to have failed, although the principal, A. C. Bigger, offered to pay two years rent—$500—in advance.[31]

The boys school was continued and its nameless condition was recognized by the lodge November 22, 1901, when a committee of George E. Seay, E. B. Wilson, and E. E. Chrisman was appointed "to select a Pythian name for our male school." [32] If the committee made a suggestion, it must have been ignored as even the committee was never again mentioned in the minutes of Rowena Lodge. The school continued without a Pythian name.

Members of Rowena Lodge were stirred by an offer made in May, 1902, by W. Y. Allen and W. G. Schamberger, Gallatin businessmen, to donate a five-acre tract of land for a school building site. The offer was made on the condition that Rowena Lodge raise $5,000 in cash within thirty days to finance, at least partially, the erection of a schoolhouse on these grounds.[33] The thirty days passed and Allen and Schamberger's challenge was not accepted, although it was discussed at length in meetings of the lodge.

After several false starts, the lodge on May 8, 1903, designated a new education committee and dispatched its members to talk to Allen and Schamberger. The deep frustration of the lodge

---

[29] *Ibid.*

[30] *Ibid.*

[31] *Ibid.*, May 27, 1900.

[32] *Rowena Lodge Minute Book, 1901-1903*, UDC Collection, Clark Chapter, Gallatin, Tenn., November 22, 1901.

[33] *Ibid.*, May 30, 1902.

with its educational activities was much in evidence in a brief entry in the minutes of the meeting of May 15, 1903: "The committee to see Allen and Schamberger made a statement of what they had done. After many motions the subject was talked to death." [34]

A week later Allen and Schamberger renewed their offer but raised the stakes. This time the lodge had to raise $10,000 within thirty days to receive their donation of five acres of land. The Knights voted at once to accept the offer but the goal was not met and on July 23 the offer was officially abandoned.[35]

Rowena Lodge turned its attention back to the school property on West Main Street and an effort was made to raise money to repair the building there. This financial campaign died a-borning and on August 31, 1903, the lodge voted to give the school property to a person or group of persons who would operate on it a "training preparatory school." [36]

When the Sumner Training School was organized in 1904, Rowena Lodge authorized its trustees to convey the old Male Seminary tract of eight acres to the new school. A payment in the amount of $2,000 was made to the lodge in the form of capital stock in the new institution. When the deed was made, a provision was included specifying that its purpose was "to aid in the promotion and building of an institution of learning known as the Sumner Training School." [37]

At last, Rowena Lodge, Knights of Pythias, Gallatin, Tennessee, was out of the school business. Its great and unfulfilled dream of the Pythian University is memorialized in a preserved section of its giant cornerstone, now removed and set for permanent display on the campus of Volunteer State Community College at Gallatin.[38]

---

[34] *Ibid.,* May 15, 1903.

[35] *Ibid.,* July 23, 1903.

[36] *Ibid.,* August 28, 31, 1903.

[37] *SCR, Deed Book #53,* p. 137.

[38] Gallatin's civic pride suffered under the impact of the failure of the Pythian College. As late as 1910, a local editor referred sarcastically to the "great Pythian College Corner Stone" as a monument that "we . . . hide . . . from the mocking eyes of our visitors by planting corn around it." Sumner County *News,* July 14, 1910.

CHAPTER VII

MIDDLE TENNESSEE STATE NORMAL COLLEGE

"SCHOOL FEVER," always quick to rise in Gallatin, soared upward in the spring of 1909 when legislation was introduced in the General Assembly at Nashville calling for the establishment of three state normal colleges, one in each grand division of the state. On May 20 the Sumner County *News* editorially challenged its readers to go to work to secure the Middle Tennessee College for Sumner County.

Public response was quick and enthusiastic. W. F. Albright, Sumner County Superintendent of Schools, endorsed the proposition on May 27 in a letter to the *News* and observed that "there is no reason why it should not be located in Gallatin, if our people will make the proper effort."

Pointing out that the availability of teacher training in such an institution would be of great help to the public schools in Sumner County, Albright declared: "It is an advantage we owe the children of the county, an opportunity that will never come again, and which must be taken at once . . . better teachers mean better schools and better education for children."

"There is also," he said, "great financial advantage to our town in the increased trade brought here by the establishment of such a school in our midst; one that would bring students from all over Middle Tennessee. There is furthermore a great moral advantage. A body of earnest young men and women with so noble a purpose can but raise the standard wherever they are."

Judge William Hall, banker and farmer, grandson of pioneer General William Hall, urged support for efforts to locate the college at Gallatin in a letter to the editor that appeared concurrently with Albright's statement. Judge Hall wrote:

Everything in and around Gallatin makes it an ideal place for such a school. There is very little time for our citizens to make up their minds as to what inducements will be offered by Sumner

97

County for the location of this school. Already the citizens of other less favored counties are preparing to enter the contest to secure the location of this school in their midst, and if our citizens will develop as much public spirit and enterprise as they manifested a few years since in an effort to get a Pythian college here, we can and will secure the location of the school here. We were very heavily handicapped in that effort, but in this such an obstacle is not to be reckoned with.

This school will be located somewhere in Middle Tennessee, and if we do not get it no one will be to blame but ourselves. Let every one interested in securing the school here talk it up to a fever heat, and let's have an enthusiastic mass-meeting of all the citizens from every district and agree upon some definite proposition to make to the State Board of Education when it shall be convened by Gov. Patterson sixty days after the passage of this bill establishing this school, to consider the location and establishment of this school.

The suggested public mass meeting was called June 3. With popular support developing throughout the county, leaders of the college movement proposed that $100,000 be raised through a county bond issue to generate seed money for the project.[1] Shortly thereafter a county-wide referendum was called to vote on a $100,000 bond issue for the college. On election day the voters, still smarting from the loss of bond issue monies voted for the Cumberland and Ohio Railroad rights of way through Sumner County sometime earlier, stayed at home in great numbers and the referendum failed to carry.[2]

Failure of the referendum served as an effective public veto of activities to locate the normal college at Gallatin. It was, the Sumner County *News* commented, a step backward for the county which in its retreat "had missed a great opportunity."[3]

The Middle Tennessee State Normal College, today Middle Tennessee State University, was subsequently located at Murfreesboro in Rutherford County.

---

[1] Sumner County *News*, June 17, 1909.
[2] *Ibid.*, July 8, 1909.
[3] *Ibid.*

BIBLIOGRAPHY

Bancroft, Frederic. *Slave Trading in the Old South*. Baltimore: J. H. Furst Company, 1931.

Biographical Directory of the American Congress, 1774-1949. Washington, D.C.: U.S. Government Printing Office, 1950.

Durham, Walter T. *Old Summer, A History of Sumner County, Tennessee, From 1805 to 1861*. Nashville: Parthenon Press, 1972.

Grimes, J. H. *History of Middle Tennessee Baptists*. Nashville: Baptist and Reflector, 1902.

History of Tennessee, From the Earliest Times to the Present; Together with an Historical and a Biographical Sketch of the Counties of Montgomery Robertson, Humphreys, Stewart, Dickson, Cheatham and Houston. Nashville: The Goodspeed Publishing Co., 1886.

Journal of Proceedings, Supreme Lodge Knights of Pythias. Vol. VIII, 1894.

Journal of Proceedings, Supreme Lodge Knights of Pythias. Vol. IX. 1896.

Minutes of the Sixtieth Anniversary of the Salem Baptist Association, September 15-16, 1882. Nashville: Messenger Office, 1882.

Minutes of the Thirtieth Annual Session of the Salem Association of United Baptists, September 17-20, 1853. McMinnville, Tennessee. The Enterprise Office, 1853.

Minutes of the Thirty-First Annual Session of the Salem Association of United Baptists, September 16-19, 1854. McMinnville, Tennessee: The Enterprise Office, 1855.

Minutes of the Thirty-Second Anniversary of the Salem Baptist Association, September 15-17, 1855. Lebanon: Herald Office, 1855.

Minutes of the Thirty-Third Anniversary of the Salem Baptist Association, September 20-22, 1856. Lebanon: Herald Office, 1856.

Minutes of the Twenty-Ninth Annual Session of the Salem Association of United Baptists, September 19-21, 1852. McMinnville, Tennessee: The Enterprise Office, 1852.

Osborne, Newell Yost. *A Select School, Mt. Union College*. Alliance, Ohio: 1967.

Read, Opie. *Mark Twain and I*. Chicago: Reilly and Lee Company, 1940.

PAMPHLETS AND BOOKLETS

Announcement of the Howard Female Institute, Gallatin, Sumner County, Tennessee, Projected by Howard Lodge No. 13, I.O.O.F., Chartered by the Legislature of Tennessee, 1856. Nashville: A. A. Stitt.

Bulletin, Howard College, 1919-1920.

The Catalog of the Officers and Pupils of Howard Female Institute For the Year 1858. Gallatin: Gray and Boyers, 1858.

Fifty-Fourth Annual Announcement of Howard Female College, Gallatin, Tennessee, 1890-91. Nashville: James T. Camp, 1890.

Fifty-Sixth Annual Announcement of Howard Female College, Gallatin, Tennessee, 1892-1893. Nashville: James T. Camp, 1892.

99

Fowler, Jo. Smith. *An Examination of a Scurrilous Pamphlet Under the Vaunting Title "Conclusive Proof that Jo. Smith Fowler is an Infidel," Written and Circulated by a Certain W. A. Harrison, His Aiders and Abettors.* Gallatin: Gray and Boyers, 1857.

Harrison, W. A. *Conclusive Proof that Mr. Jo. Smith Fowler, Principal of Gallatin Female Institute is an Infidel.* Nashville: E. Valette, 1856.

Howard College Catalog, 1914-1915.

Howard Female College Catalog, 1910-1911.

Neophogen Annual Catalog, 1877-78.

Neophogen Male and Female College, Gallatin, Tenn., Semi-Annual Catalogue, December, 1875.

Tullatuskee Commencement Program, May 21, 1908. Private Collection of Kenneth Thomson.

NEWSPAPERS AND MAGAZINES

The Bud of Thought. Edited by the Young Ladies of Howard Female Institute. Gallatin: John S. Ward, 1860.

Chattanooga *Daily Times.*

The College Pen.

Gallatin *Examiner.*

Gallatin *Journal.*

Gallatin *Semi-Weekly News.*

Gallatin *Tennessean.*

Gallatin *Union.*

Howard College Argus.

Hartsville *Vidette.*

Memphis *Appeal-Avalanche.*

Nashville *Banner.*

Nashville *Daily Centre-State American.*

Nashville *Daily Union.*

Nashville *Union.*

The Nation (New York).

National Banner and Nashville Whig.

Sumner County *News.*

The Weekly Pythian Period (Nashville).

PUBLIC RECORDS

Succession of Isaac Frankin, Seventh Judicial District Court. West Feliciana, Louisiana, circa 1852.

Sumner County Records
   SCR, Deed Books #16, #21, #23, #31, #41, #43, #46, #53, #82, #84, #95.
   SCR, Chancery Minute Books #17 and #18.

Tennessee Acts, 1835-36; 1843-44; 1847-48; 1855-56; 1857-58.

United States Postal Records. National Archives and Records Service.

BIBLIOGRAPHY

UNPUBLISHED MATERIALS

George W. Wynne Papers, Tennessee Historical Society Collections.

Minutes of Board of Education of Tullatuskee Normal School at Bethpage. Private Collection of Mrs. Virginia Key Wemyss.

Minutes of Howard Lodge No. 13, I.O.O.F., Minute Book 1885-1905. Private Collection of John Garrott.

Rowena Lodge Minute Book, 1896-1900. UDC Collection, Clark Chapter, Gallatin, Tenn.

Rowena Lodge Minute Book, 1901-1903. UDC Collection, Clark Chapter, Gallatin, Tenn.

MAP

Map of Sumner County, Tennessee. D. C. Beers and Company, Philadelphia, Pennsylvania, 1878.

INDEX